CW00448291

Yearning to Breathe Free

A Community Journal of 2020

Editors:

Mary Susan Gast, Mary Eichbauer

Copyright © 2022 Benicia Literary Arts
All Rights Reserved

No part of this book may be reproduced, transmitted or stored in any form or by any means, electronic or mechanical, without the express written permission of the publisher, except for brief quotations embodied in critical articles and reviews. Upon publication, all rights to individual works revert to their authors.

ISBN: 978-1-7354999-2-5
Library of Congress Control Number 2021924467

Published by Benicia Literary Arts
P.O. Box 1903
Benicia, CA 94510
www.benicialiteraryarts.org

Benicia Literary Arts encourages reading and writing in the community by producing events, creating a community of writers and readers, encouraging their development, and publishing works of high quality in all genres.

Editors: Mary Susan Gast and Mary Eichbauer
Cover Photo: Dimitar Donovski at unsplash.com
Book Design: Deborah L. Fruchey
Photo credits: Man on bench, page 32, Daniel Jensen at unsplash.com
Back cover: Christopher Michael at Wikimedia Commons
Thanks for additional help from Sherry Sheehan and Roger Straw

Thanks to the *Benicia Herald* for publishing the ongoing column, "Going the Distance," and for granting permission to use collected material from that column for this anthology.

The materials below were previously published and are used with the permission of the authors:

"They Propped the Dead Man Up: an Allegory," Sandra Anfang, first published in *The New Verse News* (newversenews.blogspot.com, October 7, 2020)

"Dark Matter," Jeannette DesBoine, originally published in *Breaking News 45* (OCO Independent Publishing, 2017).

"Seasons of Grief," Jeannette DesBoine, originally published in *Disaster Revisited* (Create Space Publishing, 2015).

"An Abundance of Caution, April 2020," Joanne Jagoda, first published in *My Runaway Hourglass* (Poetica Publishing Company, 2020).

Copyrighted material, used by permission:

Walter Brueggemann, excerpt from *Finally Comes the Poet* (Augsburg Fortress Press, 1989). Used by permission of the publisher.

"Days Pass and the Years Vanish," from *Gates of Prayer: A New Union Prayerbook*, copyright © 1975 by the Central Conference of American Rabbis. Used by permission of the Central Conference of American Rabbis. All rights reserved.

Mary Susan Gast, excerpts from *Redemption Songs—A 21st Century Descant on the Psalms*, ©2001. Used by permission of the author.

"I Dream a World," from *The Collected Poems of Langston Hughes* by Langston Hughes, edited by Arnold Rampersad with David Roessel, Associate Editor, copyright © 1994 by the Estate of Langston Hughes. Used by permission of Alfred A. Knopf, an imprint of the Knopf Doubleday Publishing Group, a division of Penguin Random House LLC. All rights reserved.

"Let America Be America Again," from *The Collected Poems of Langston Hughes* by Langston Hughes, edited by Arnold Rampersad with David Roessel, Associate Editor, copyright ©1994 by the Estate of Langston Hughes. Used by permission of Alfred A. Knopf, an imprint of the Knopf Doubleday Publishing Group, a division of Penguin Random House LLC. All rights reserved.

Ada Maria Isasi-Diaz, excerpt from *Mujerista Theology* (Orbis Books, 1996). Used by permission of the publisher.

Carolyn Randall Williams, excerpt from "You Want a Confederate Monument?" From *The New York Times*. ©2020 The New York Times Company. All rights reserved. Used under license.

Statistics on cumulative U.S. COVID deaths

COVID-19 Data Repository by the Center for Systems Science and Engineering (CCSE) at Johns Hopkins University," *Our World in Data*, ourworldindata.org/coronavirus/country/united-states?country=~USA#what-is-the-cumulative-number-of-confirmed-deaths, as accessed February 21, 2021.

"We will tell the stories of how we overcome,
and we'll understand it better by and by."

— From the hymn, "By and By," by Charles Tindley

Table of Contents

Preface

On Sunday, March 23, 2020, I sent an email to Galen Kusic, editor of the *Benicia Herald*, our town's thrice-weekly newspaper. "As the fears grow around the coronavirus and tensions increase about 'shelter in place,' I've been imagining a column to appear in each edition of the *Herald* that would voice and speak to the fears, tensions, inspirations, hopes, and oddities we are experiencing." Galen responded with encouragement.

Later that week I called for contributions to the column "Going the Distance," to offer strength, hope, and solidarity in a time of social distancing. The first column ran on April 1, with the guy-on-the-bench-looking-over-the-strait logo. Poets, writers, and people who had never previously written poetry or prose for publication sent their material. Not every submission was published, but everyone who submitted was published at least once. Giving voice to the community was one of the purposes of the column. We also sought and included some material from sources beyond our time frame and geographic area for deepened perspective and insight. Writings were selected to "pair" with one another in a column, to contrast with or enhance each other in content or style. (I eventually learned that this is called "curating" the submissions.)

Around us lives and livelihoods were shutting down. "The craving for normalcy growls like an empty stomach," Lois Request wrote in early April. Despite our isolation, events contrived a widened awareness of the shared human condition. We could not maintain a distance between ourselves and the manifestations of embedded racism, economic hardship, climate crisis, and threats to democracy. Jerry Bolick framed this awareness in the question, "Whose Shelter? Which Virus?"

So, on Juneteenth, the guy-on-the-bench logo gave way to Lady Liberty, masked up, lighting the way for all who are "yearning," in every sense, "to breathe free." To breathe free of all the chokeholds that threaten us. As individuals, as communities, as a nation, as a planet.

Yearning to Breathe Free became the title for the book you are holding, the collection of the newspaper columns that ran from April 1 to Election Day 2020. May we all read this chronicle of our shared history to remember and to learn. I commend it to you with deep appreciation for all we have gone through, all we face, and all who have committed to go the distance together.

Mary Susan Gast, Editor
Benicia Poet Laureate

Foreword

When the first reports of COVID-19 infections in China circulated in January 2020, many Americans experienced a brief unease, before going on as usual with their daily lives. By the end of that month, the brewing crisis was harder to ignore—in China, 200 people were confirmed dead, and the first cases arrived in the U.S. Restricted international travel quickly followed, then travelers' quarantines, COVID-stricken cruise ships trapped off the coasts of American cities, massive disease outbreaks in elder-care homes. How bad could this get? How long would it last? Could this disease be controlled? As questions multiplied, the fear grew harder to ignore.

On March 19, 2020, California became the first U.S. state to issue a blanket stay-at-home order. From one day to the next, the tenor and rhythm of our lives changed, and new realities took root: deserted streets; closed shops and theaters; shortages of food, bottled water, and—absurdly—toilet paper. Millions of people isolated at home with their immediate families, disconnected from friends and family, left alone with their own thoughts and anxieties.

In Benicia, California, a town of 27,000 on the Carquinez Strait, things transpired much as they did in other small American towns. Formerly crowded coffee shops, bars, and restaurants were shuttered. Normally friendly people walking their dogs began stepping into the street when they passed another person to avoid possible contagion. Family activities like picnicking in the parks disappeared. People seemed to scowl suspiciously at each other, but, even if they were smiling, it was impossible to tell because of the masks covering their lower faces. First white painters' masks, or blue surgical ones, later, N-95s. People got creative, sewing their own out of cheerful scraps of fabric. Neighbors left masks on neighbors' porches, along with books, baskets of cookies, or casseroles.

Face-to-face human contact melted away, replaced by greetings from afar; by phone calls, emails or texts; by objects left on porches. Neighborhoods organized socially distanced sing-alongs or pot-banging sessions, often meant to express thanks to first responders who were putting their lives on the line.

In the face of these sudden, unprecedented changes, Mary Susan Gast—poet, theologian, human rights activist—recognized the need for her community to rediscover its voice. The first installment of her series "Going the Distance" appeared in the Benicia Herald on April 1 and featured poems by two local poets.

Right on the heels of COVID-19, the murder of George Floyd in Minneapolis on May 25 sent ripples of outrage through this already beleaguered country. The Black Lives Matter movement blossomed, shredding white complacency and forcing many to a horrified consciousness of pernicious racism and the perilous realities of Black Americans' lives. Many people responded to Mr. Floyd's horrifying death—to which we all became stunned witnesses—expressing their horror, anger, mourning, and guilt; asking questions; demanding change. "Going the Distance" expanded its scope to meet this need, too.

Every Wednesday, Friday, and Sunday since April 1, Mary Susan's column appeared, featuring personal responses to the crises that wracked this nation in 2020, as well as some that were present long before COVID-19 made hermits of us all: racism, inequality, climate change, political divisiveness. (Although the column still continues to appear in the Benicia newspaper, this collection, the *Yearning to Breathe Free* anthology, cuts off on Sunday, November 1, 2020, the last date the paper was issued before the 2020 election.)

Collected here, you will read the personal responses of a community, presented largely as they appeared, day by day, during the thick of uncertainty and doubt. They stand as a historical record from one small corner of America, a raw, unmediated testimony to hope and fear, anger and despair, inspired by events as they unfolded.

In addition to their function as historical artifacts, we hope these personal responses will serve as an impetus to discussion in our own community and elsewhere, not as a goad to disagreement, but as a visceral reminder of the tragedies we have collectively experienced, whose ramifications have not, as of this writing, fully played themselves out.

Mary Eichbauer, Editor-in-Chief
Benicia Literary Arts

Two Weeks Ago

my windows were pass-throughs,
outside inviting play in faithful
light of freedom

undistracted frolic
splendor in little fragments
costs nothing to sing in this space
now each day comes with a price
virus unfolding like a crumbled map
roads to new paths uncertain
powerful   pivotal   ploughs

drops into the unknown
stops any hope.

Stay in   social distance
masks to conceal   gloves to ensure
eyes reveal hesitation to look
beyond the fear

my mind wants to block
locked like my windows are now
grief begins to cover
as I huddle underneath a fleece blanket.

Two weeks ago
my world now memorized by my heart
must remember   must not forget
this is where faith begins.

Suzanne Bruce

Corona

Corona,
halo of death—
a crown
no one wants to wear.

We isolate ourselves in fear—
give up trains and planes—
the touch of a hand,
the embrace of a friend.

We hide under blankets
in unmarked tents,
in the last room
that has a view of the sunset.

The natural world continues—
a hummingbird quivers in the air,
a tree blossoms into luscious green,
a warm breeze rustles the butterflies awake.

Standing 6 feet away
from someone else,
I watch the sun
disappear behind the trees—
each of us crowned
with its light.

Johanna Ely

Total U.S. deaths from COVID-19: 6662

Friday, April 3, 2020
Surviving

Tuesdays With Helen

Helen is my closest friend of fifty years. We raised our kids in tandem sharing many heartbreaks and happy moments. The Covid-19 virus is invading our lifelong friendship. Helen lives in Walnut Creek. She can't really see very well anymore and she can't drive. She was my Tuesday date. I would go to Walnut Creek, take her to doctor's appointments and shopping; we'd get pedicures, and go to the movies. Before coronavirus.

Now everything is closed except the grocery stores. Because of physical limitations we can't walk far; sitting outside is not a great option either. The cold makes us stiff; we both have arthritis. Symptoms that often plague me at non-virus times, happening now, raise the question of whether my aching joints, sinus headaches, red itchy eyes, or lack of energy are a threat to friends. These are the kind of symptoms seniors tend to get with Covid-19. And Helen's adult son lives with her. He goes out and who knows where he goes? And what he might bring home? So many questions.

In these difficult times I am left with two choices. Grocery shopping with her, or not.

Here's the rub. She's a very tactile person, a hugger. And she likes to pick everything up, touch it, squeeze it, read the labels, expiration dates, etc. She carries a magnifying glass with her. It takes forever. She's lonely and friendly and likes to talk to people. People respecting the six-foot physical distance aren't as receptive these days. They want to get in and get out. I have offered to order food for her online and have it sent. She has no technology in her home besides the jitterbug phone I got her so she could call from wherever for help if needed. She is not receptive to more technology.

I am torn up. If it was a family member, like my mother or sister, I would just put my foot down and insist that she accept food ordering and delivery. But this being her only opportunity to move among the living, I can't discourage it. Her son still takes her to the store. It is still an ordeal.

Beth Grimm

The Way of Balance

In everything evil, the potential for good; in everything good, the potential for evil. We live by the grace of the Great Mystery and the goodness of one human being toward another.

Ojibwe teaching

Total U.S. deaths from COVID-19: 9600

Orchestra

Fingers tap dry rhythms
on instruments in need of tuning
trumpets blare sour notes
out of tune cellos squeal
violins and violas whine
flute-stops fill with spit
no sound escapes
French horns blare discord
triangles without hammers
bells lacking clappers
pianos with covers shut
gather dust, keys silent
harps with broken strings,
stretched beyond endurance.
We long for harmony,
a return to a daily symphony.
We wait for a conductor
who knows the score.

Louise Moises

The Last Banana

Today I bought the last banana at Raley's,
somebody left it, not on the wire hanging
rack, but above it, undersize as it was, on the
small display shelf, a token offering of
benevolence perhaps in the "Shelter in
place" chaos that currently infects our
planet. I don't understand the communist
state whose occupants must eat bats, living
upside down in infected caves or doorways,
is this the measure of superlative
governance? Are these Chinese-FDA
regulated and inspected bats? Range-free?
Gluten-free? No MSG? Or are they the scrub
of edibles, Coronavirus-infected, overlooked
for millennia by the non-existence of an
imposter Donald Trump-equivalent,
closing down the Chinese EPA (if it ever
existed) or are they Tariff-complicated,
proving something to somebody in the
aftermath of who delayed public disclosure
the most, or the longest for whose political
expedience? Who will win the Tariff Wars or
lose the most innocent, hapless residents in
deaths to this first pandemic of this
generation? Bananas and bats and Banana
Republics, the countries continue, shelter
in place.

Peter Bray

The Question

I look askance, paste on a smile;
Heart produces a flutter.
My brain flits to a different place,
one I had never known before.
Questions cluster around the heart...next?
I ask.
Not today. Tomorrow?
The uncertainty creeps deeper and I only
have passed one walker.

Jan Radesky

Total U.S. deaths from COVID-19: 12,780

Corona Pantoum*

I am waiting for the death of coronavirus
I am waiting for sheltering to end
I am waiting for the *ahas!* of epidemiologists
with their beautiful nomenclature

I am waiting for sheltering to end
I am waiting for the streets to fill with dogs
and children
with their beautiful nomenclature
I am waiting for the lost embrace

I am waiting for the streets to fill
        with dogs and children
I am waiting through unnamed weeks and
        months
I am waiting for the lost embrace
for the great re-leveling.

I am waiting through unnamed weeks and
        months
for disinfecting to end and singing to start
for the great re-leveling
I am waiting with taut muscles

for disinfecting to end and singing to start
& for the water to be filled with fish and
        swimmers
I am waiting with taut muscles
for the peal of the dismissal bell

& for the water to be filled with fish and
        swimmers
I am waiting for the death of coronavirus
for the peal of the dismissal bell
I am waiting for the ahas! of
epidemiologists.

Sandra Anfang

*The pantoum is a poetic form that features a
series of interwoven lines.

Streets I Have Never Walked Before

Silent now
Familiar but still

The sound of a human voice
alerts me
Where is it? Where are they?
Am I safe?

The patter of a thousand voices,
footfalls halted.
By something we can't see
Science fiction

Across the street a mute baseball field
No cracking bats
No one on base
No runs, no outs
Nothing

The craving for normalcy
growls like an empty stomach.

Lois Requist

Total U.S. deaths from COVID-19: 19,282

Camp Corona, USA!!

They say familiarity breeds contempt.
If you subscribe to that philosophy,
then please, allow me to vent.

To be different is to be blessed.
I mean what if we were all the same,
can you imagine the bigger mess?

Imagine much more madness
than we currently have now.
Just like the Corona Virus, it would manifest
            numerically.
I mean wow!!

I bet you couldn't stay here.
No matter the price.
And would you really want to?
Even to save your own life.

The simple differences
that we fight about.
Those apparent idiosyncs.
All these things would pale.
And we would begin to think.
Think about how precious life is
and what past truths we might revamp.

To quote Dr. King before he died,
"We're all in the same Camp."
A camp that can fold up anytime
reminding us of our fragility;
the obvious and the sublime.

Out of sight is not always out of mind!
Is What I'm trying to VENT
I hope I got you thinking, America

While the CORONA VIRUS does its best to
tear down your tent.

Bobby Richardson

It's a Little Like Riding the Rapids

Just hang on.

It's a little like
riding the rapids
down by Whiskey Flats
bumping over rocks
in an old inner tube
no time to think
in the foamy whitewater
of the Feather River.

Just hang on.

It might get a little rough
you may get some bruises
but you'll be okay.

Just hang on.

Keep your eyes downriver
wait for the big pool
the slow smooth current
where you can drift
in the sun.

Just hang on.

James Fredenburg

Total U.S. deaths from COVID-19: 23,692

9

Time

There is no difference between days. No nights. No high or low tide. No voices in the background. No faces that smile. No light or dark.

There is no motion. No sound of prancing feet. No traceable heartbeat. No pulse. No rhythm. No blues.

There is no rock and roll. No rap or hip-hop. No classics on radio waves. Only Alerts coming from who knows where.

There are thoughts. Haunting and promising simultaneously. Fear and hope mixed in the same sterile petri dish.

And there is sun. Which, no matter what, shows up every morning letting Time know that Earth still lives; Tomorrow exists; and so shall we.

Jeannette DesBoine

Menace

Amoral as a freight train,
Unremorseful as a vapor trail,
Airborne touchborne virus,
Silent invader.

Microbe magnified to reveal
        a deranged posy,
        a psychedelic Telstar,
robbing us of smell and taste
clawing at our lungs.

Mary Susan Gast

A Space

the morning light
lays on my eyes
reminds me to awaken wide
I twist under my pile of blankets
my toes cold, my head and heart warmed

I remember
I am in my sister's house
her family room-office converted to a space for me
I have no work because of Covid-19
I am a makeup artist, face painter and entertainer. a poet

decided in two days to move
left all my furniture behind
I'm over 60, no kids or husband, just a cute little doggie named Zach

I'm giving myself a fighting chance
my sister needs one too
she's a single mom with a mortgage in the San Francisco Bay
we will grow food in her yard wild jungle
we'll yoga in the living room
and party via zoom
we'll distance
wash our hands more times in one day than we used to in a week

My emotions go so far up and so far down
they're hard to keep up with
I'm glad to be with my sister

Diana Tenes

Total U.S. deaths from COVID-19: 27,682

Shards of Days (Daze?)

During the first few weeks, it took seven days to do one day's worth of tasks. A single day could have several tasks (laundry, bills, organizing spaghetti inventory), but that one day was dropped on the ground and shattered like a bath bomb...shards that broke, splintered and spread out over seven days.

Every day had unfinished jobs in it...not one task got started and finished in a single 24-hour period. On any given day, you'd see open doors, open cabinets in mid-cleaning, open flaps on my vitamin pillbox in mid-fill. Open folders in my brain, preoccupied with worries about people on the front lines.

Dishwasher door hanging open, not sure if dishes were coming or going. Washing machine door open; I added soap and walked away without starting it. Salad cut up, fork standing upright in a carrot, waiting for bite number two. It looked like the rapture had happened, our house people sucked away in mid-task.

And the *Sounds!* I'm now in tune with my home life. I can tell what my husband is drinking (hot tea), and out of which cup (large plastic yellow Dickey's cup) by how he swallows. I listen to how long and deep our cat is digging in the litter box, and know exactly what she's about to deliver.

I don't like that I know this. I don't even recognize myself anymore.

I said to my husband, I'm turning over a new leaf for our upcoming week. I'm going to get up early, shower, make my own coffee and take care of a large to-do list so that I can think straight. Last week I lost the plot. I am going to let last week go. It just didn't...It just didn't...

My husband finishes my thought because he gets me: "Last week *just didn't.*"

Yes, and this week just might.

Sherilee Hoffmann

If Breath Is a Journey

The moon persists,
still goes through her phases,
and the earth revolves,
ever in rotation,
but human life on the planet
pauses in place
in a frantic effort to save it.
If breath is a journey
between birth and death
where new hope is
carved by inspiration,
then chisel, inscribe,
whittle, engrave it,
each gift, each lesson,
each challenge,
each celebration,
even though even those,
in the final exhalation,
will be lost to the soft moss
that conquers broken pavement.

Ramona Lappier

Total U.S. deaths from COVID-19: 34,731

Pandemic

(An Acrostic)

Please, I
Ask
Nervously,
Don't we know that this
Experience
Mimics
Incidents from earlier
Centuries?

Perhaps exact
Answers
Never arrive,
Denying me
Examples of
Meaning
In this Covid-19
Crisis that simultaneously

Provides
An opportunity to
Navigate my life more
Deliberately than
Ever before, while
Making self-
Isolation
Courageously, curiously contagious.

Sherry Sheehan

Couplets of Coping I

I spend twenty seconds washing my hands
And twenty more checking for swollen glands.

So please step aside when you see me approach,
Teach this to your children like you're their coach.

The thing that will save and unite us all
Is the distance we put between us till fall.

Evie Groch

Sheltering in Place

Standing in the sun on the balcony
the hummingbird feeder busy with birds
A woman walks by with a fluffy white dog
carrying a little brown paper bag
I call out "hello"
In my isolation I am safe
but I miss the chance for
conversations with strangers
that brought me so much joy
that filled my long life
that taught me much
She and dog stopped
looking upward
She said "Hello
See I got this at the liquor store
to make into sanitizing spray"
She pulls out a small bottle
"Clear All it's 100% alcohol
to mix with my aloe vera plant
and vitamin E"
The dog tugs to move on
Carefully she puts her treasure
back in the bag
She is gone
I need some sanitizer
but it's too late to ask her if it leaves a smell
If the sun is shining
maybe she will pass again tomorrow

Nina Serrano

Total U.S. deaths from COVID-19: 38,995

Walking, Petaluma

Wind chimes.
Comforting and simultaneously lonely.
My dog and I walk alone.
Together, yet alone. Noticing.
Homes, streets, cars, others walking.
Yet mostly empty silence. Wind. Chimes.
In the last ten or so days, (really only ten?)
a shift as I walk,
and cross streets or change direction,
mostly, not from apprehension,
but to respect the space of others
either the young family, the older couple,
who perhaps
pushing the stroller, or walking their dog,
cannot change direction as quickly,
so I cross away from them.
Others do the same for me.
But here and there, where we were smiling
and offering a friendly greeting
only a week or two ago,
now more silence.
Folks retreating into their own
thoughts, own heads, own safety.

Passing the Creamery,
still steaming, working,
emanating its somewhat comforting
sour milk aroma.
Workers there, still collecting the milk
from our hard-working cows and dairy folk.
Processing it into cheese—so solidly
delicious, nutritious.
How can that smell impress itself upon my
psyche in that way,
make me feel so grateful
for its familiar presence?
Thirty-five years of passing it by, perhaps,
and what is familiar and unchanged

is somewhat comforting
The high school. I used to teach there
two weeks ago,
before learning distantly began.
Passing the courts, tennis and basketball,
I see two blonde brothers
lose the basketball over the fence.
It bounces toward the street.
A man on the other side of the chain link
pulls down both sleeves,
retrieves the ball,
without actually touching it,
and tosses it back to the boys.

Krista O'Connor

Hope

Hope,
Saltier than
saccharine optimism,
More like courage.
Facing the facts,
Forging a future.

Mary Susan Gast

Total U.S. deaths from COVID-19: 42,967

A Perfect Day

Morning streams through windows
Spotted with fossilized raindrops
Front doors open to a rush of clean sweet air
Dog walkers, phone talkers,
    coffee drinkers, skateboarders,
Young couples and old friends
    populate First Street
The strait glints silver on blue
As fishermen bait their hooks
At the start of a perfect day.

Home delivery trucks dart through intersections
Pedestrians stroll past darkened shop windows
Navigating careful detours around one another
Diners carry out house specials
    from empty restaurants
Big kids roam from block to block
Looking for diversions
Small ones trail behind preoccupied parents
Craving the customary ice cream stop

We fear the danger
We hope for safety
We reach for each other
With eyes, smiles, nods, greetings
More than before

A willowy figure outlined against the evening sky
Lifts bow to strings
A dozen spectators stand apart
Swaying together
Sing Hallelujah
At the end of a perfect day.

Kathleen Herrmann

The Audacity of Water

Today on my walk
I heard the trickle of water.
It's funny how its sound moves me
to do anything I choose.
The frigid wetness tickles my bones
when they just want to be still.

Mornings when I want to stay in,
mostly because depression
slowly creeped in, water calms.

Worry, Panic, & Fear
of the unknown slowly melts away
See the pine trees wrestle with the wind
The way my baby blows the wishing flower
And watches bubbles flow by
Although we are dying, nature still lives
And that's a reason to hope again

Aqueila M. Lewis-Ross

Total U.S. deaths from COVID-19: 50,165

Pathogen

The new coronavirus hides invisibly
  in droplets,
Respiratory droplets.
Deadly, once inside our bodies,
It collides, crashing into cells and guiding
Its perfect replication;
Its skillful annihilation.
Collaborative minds unite
  to outsmart the virus.
It thinks; it communicates; it eavesdrops;
it destroys—
Its molecular language, its messaging
  a mystery;
The virus seems to control its own destiny.
Can we control ours?

Mad, feverish push for scientists worldwide
To develop a vaccine against COVID-19,
The disease the virus causes.
And world-class Nobel Committees
  take note,
While major breakthroughs await discovery,
Just outside Humanity's reach.
The world is slowly learning to share,
Slowly learning to care.
Trying again and again, once more
To mount a strong defense.
Meanwhile, the deadly pathogen lives on—
Unrestrained.

Nancy Tolin

What Remains is Love

In these days of quarantine
we mourn the loss of many things
from people who succumbed too soon
to jobs and hobbies we can no longer do.

We miss our friends' warm embrace.
We miss seeing our loved one's smiling face.
Though these times are unusual indeed,
we all sit together in solidarity
with nurses, doctors, and employees
that keep turning the wheels of society.

So to you, my friends, I raise my glass.
We will survive. This, too shall pass.
We will get through this alone together.
We will find new activities to weather
this newest storm of uncertainty.

As certain as the birds' morning song
the sun still shines despite all that's wrong.
One day our lives shall again bloom
for what remains is our love
even within the darkest gloom.

D.L. Lang

Total U.S. deaths from COVID-19: 54,824

"Ganando"
(The Treatment of Trachoma with Sulfanilamide)

Won!
Community Verified!
Ganado, ganado vacuno, vacas
Ganado, hacienda
Stuffed stock;
Vástago, tallo, tronco, pie, roda, caña
Valores, existencia, caldo, capital, ganado, ...
Tronco.
Sixty-one hunters
Were chosen by lot
A run
Of 5 to 10 miles
In place,
When packages of cigarettes
Came floating down
From the sky
In little parachutes
A pageant announcement
Frills-no-ills
... Can't explain it
Milk bottle on the doorstep
Curbside hello!
Lone Ranger sings through her mask
Yes!
I don't have
That
Memory
Justice this
Memory
Of future yester'to'-day
A mile ago
Storm shutters
Braced
For the calm.
As a boy of 12
Ridden by pony express
Delivering
Is a miracle drug
There will be peace in Chandler tonight
Flags oft repaired and flaxen,

... Stiff ... waxen; with belief
Hope is what makes any soup
From nothing
Anything
Will do.

It is a beautiful Spring day
Here in Ganando
And looking out
It's a heck of a, ...
Wonderful view,
... Just after Easter
... Eggs painted
"429"
For the next; ...
Holiday.

Tom Stanton

Fighting Coronavirus

Battle internalized, with
    wrenching chills
    enervating fever
    desperate fatigue.
Battle externalized, in the
tamped-down status quo
  of physical distancing,
daily grit required
  to deliver essential services,
hand-to-hand extreme risk combat
  with the force and forces of COVID-19,
while enduring, persisting,
surviving, together,
    tendering lifelines of compassion,
    improvising girders of support.

Mary Susan Gast

Total U.S. deaths from COVID-19: 57,931

The Lesson

...and if this current harshness in life is to
teach us a lesson,
then what can we learn?
And the answer came out of
a newly crystal sky
reflected in the clear blue of the water
below...

Tread gently upon me
  taking only what you need
  without having to own more
listen to the melody of the trees and the wind
  hear the quiet peeps of a common bird
  letting it be a sweet song in your heart
observe the cycles of life
  from the microscopic to the magnificent
  that existed long before
  your cycle came to be,
see the power of earth's natural forces
  shaping the environment
  long before you made
  your human marks on the planet
know that this is not your world to possess
  but you were born in it and of it
  and must dwell on it in harmony
realize that if you wish
  to dominate and conquer
  the tiniest microbe
  can bring you to your knees.

...and if we are to be humbled,
then what can we value?
And the answer echoed across a world
of empty streets, plazas, and bazaars.....

Learn to be content with what you can
  hold in your hands
  see in your cupboards
  or feel in your places of softness

let the beauty of an art piece
  or splendor of a song
  no matter how simple
  take residence in your soul
never underestimate
  the healing power of a laugh
  the innocence of a child
  or the importance of a hug
tend to your garden of relationships
  for as they grow and bloom
  so will your inner strength
let gratitude wash over your being to
  speak the love others need to hear
  while they can still do so
and when the darkness comes
  know how precious it is
  simply to feel safe.

Katrina Monroe

Perspective

Overslept!
Probably a good thing...
Less time for cabin fever.

Jeannette DesBoine

Total U.S. deaths from COVID-19: 64,078

Calling to the World

Standing in this space,
Not knowing what to do,
Nor what could be happening.
Is this it?
Is this the end?
Will this be extinct?
Is there a message through this all?
Is this God's doings?
There is no way,
No way this is true,
For the birds still chirp,
The leaves still blow,
The grass still sways
And the mountains still snow.

The way it all shows,
Is the way it all goes,
For the Earth has undergone
The worst it can,
Or possibly not at all,
The numbers still climb,
But the wind still chimes.

This is not the way,
Not the way it should be.
It makes no sense,
For the sun still shines,
The rain still falls,
And the cat still crawls.

There will be no end,
For the Earth has undergone
The ten worst things,
Although that is,
These things,
These things that have moved the world,
These things that are called,
Pandemics.

Bella Vaca

A Cure...

Where did this virus come from?
From the sky, or the earth or from someone?
Is it from a demographic persuasion?
Africans, Spaniards, Europeans or Asians.

We are all from the same seed-of-life,
The doctors see red when we bleed-our cry.
Even though social distancing keeps us apart,
Loneliness ought to enhance our hearts!

The rich will get a huge tax break,
While the poor are forced to stay in their place.
Taxpayers received a small stimulus check,
While small businesses haven't gotten anything yet.

There's talk of states
        opening-up their doors,
The arguments loom,
        "what would they do that for?"
Many are mandated to,
        the "stay at home order" in place,
In public—6 feet breathing space,
        with a mask on their face!

I hope CDC perfect the new vaccination.
To provide A CURE for everybody,
        in every nation!
Cause we are all God's creation...
Only He can save us!
From this virus....

Mary "Lady-D" Brown

Total U.S. deaths from COVID-19: 68,265

Bees

The day the bees were to come she could hardly sit still. They were on their way and she was sure they were smashed into a box and sitting in a hot delivery van somewhere between her home and the apiary. She hoped they would be OK. The shipping notification had arrived in her email that morning. Their new home was ready; the spring flowers blooming in welcome. "Stop pacing," her husband joked, having lived through the child-like Christmas morning excitement she always had around plants and animals. They brought her such joy and had been her friends along the 63 year long path she was on. It was the pure non-judging "being" of the plants and animals that drew her in. Rational, logical, totally understandable behaviors, if you spent time learning amongst them as she had. Such a joy from the early years of living with constant judging that had made her doubt her every move and thought. "OK, I'll stop, I know, I'll go out and check the top bar hive, or make up some sugar water to tide them over when they get here."

The day was perfect. Life had ground to a virtual and almost physical stop. In the big world just outside the front door, a pandemic was raging. The Shelter-In-Place order so wisely brought down by the Governor had been going now for 3 weeks. The virus seemed to be showing signs of being controlled and kept away from its human victims by this societal shift, but hiding out here in her home had forced a simple, prioritized living that felt in a very strange way, peaceful and calm. She felt grateful to be able to Shelter-In-Place at all, knowing much of the world couldn't and didn't have the blessings she had. There was guilt with that thought. The masks she made to donate, the staying at home to stay out of the way of the virus and the people dealing with it, felt like tiny, tiny things in this world of such great sorrow and catastrophe.

Surrendering to this and taking some tiny steps and just staying sort of sane, became huge things in a world turned upside down.

The day the bees were to arrive happened to coincide with the local surge in the virus. She could feel her whole neighborhood and the broader community around her, peering out their windows, watching the news, waiting, waiting to see if the sacrifices of isolation and quarantine and stopping the hard-wired connectedness of hugs and un-masked smiles would work; would be worth the loss of such a treasured part of our humanness. The signs seemed good, but there was enough hubris and "touch-wood" superstition to not want to start celebrating yet. The bees were her way of bringing a little bit of sweetness to this bitter, sad time. The sound of the delivery truck in front of her house broke into her thoughts and she ran to greet the sweetness.

Deborah Morrison

Couplets of Coping II

Out of nowhere comes a plague
       with an inconspicuous start,
Now pandemic shivers
       keep us six feet apart.

Evie Groch

> *Total U.S. deaths from COVID-19: 71,166*

Wednesday, May 6, 2020
What it's like now

Before (COVID-19)

I took a long whiff of yesterday,
So I could remember
what it was like before—
When the wind whispered my name
rain danced upon my shoulders

I tapped into nature's beauty
I once took for granted—
Flowers that turn their petals
To a laughing sun
Trees that recolor earth

Now inside, during a recent spring,
Effects of a virus
I inhaled freshly mowed grass
against an uncertain sky,
but the scent is not the same.

Juanita Martin

The Walk

The moment I stepped outside,
　　it was a lot brighter
　　and smelled so fresh.
As I kept walking,
　　the trees looked a lot greener
　　and a lot taller.
I was so surprised by all this color
　　but maybe it was just me
　　who hasn't taken a walk
　　for a long time.
I loved how the Earth was looking
　　and would love to do it again.

Ryleigh Todd

One That Just Wouldn't Quit

Our forty-ninth was to be a modest date,
A forty-ninth year, a minor fete:
A fine meal with offspring
An aloha slack-key concert guitar thing…

But alas, it was not to be.
No small celebration,
No outing, no feast.
No, nothing at all,
No simple date to recall…

Our forty-ninth was cancelled
By a stay-at-home order.
The medical experts
Warned of death,
The virus, infection, the world under siege,
For forty-nine days or more perhaps,
Pandemic days!

But no, our forty-ninth
Will sure be remembered
As the one that would not quit,
The time together
An anniversary that lasted weeks and months
In each other's way,
In each other's arms,
In each other's precious time and space,
A house full of you and me.

Our forty-ninth,
The anniversary that went viral.
We'll never forget.

Roger Straw

Total U.S. deaths from COVID-19: 77,057

A Death on the Sidelines

Victor died last week,
Of lupus, not COVID-19,
In a V.A. hospital in Washington State.
No friends switched sentinel duty at his bedside,
No family hustled in from Iowa,
All hostage to the killer microbe.

Victor's neighbor is a nurse
Working in that hospital,
Above and beyond her shift.
She stayed with him
As he left the realm of time and space.
She is, bi-vocationally and indisputably,
        an angel.

In strictly theological terms,
Angels are messengers from God.
In totally realistic terms,
Angels are envoys from the great Love
        at the core of the universe,
        at the heart of our hearts.
Angels, these desolate days, often appear
Adorned in masks and ill-fitting gowns,
But there is no mistaking them.

"She stayed with him,
        and she brought us comfort,"
Victor's mother told me on the phone,
Through her quarantined heartbreak.

Mary Susan Gast

Essential Worker

On the way to work again
To do this noble deed

But it is really just my job
To work and keep us free

On my shift at work again
I hope I make it home

They say that I'm essential
But I just feel alone

If I make it home tonight
I'll pray for just one more

And just maybe one day
Tears of joy we'll pour

On the road to work again
I pray for all those souls

I think about the future
Who knows what it will hold

The world that we all live in
The roads that some must travel

It's in my heart to make it
Before it all unravels

On the way to work again

Galen Kusic

Total U.S. deaths from COVID-19: 80,727

Roses

Wildly profligate
Red heads open up
And then—buds cloaked
In some mysterious beaded
  embroidery stitch,
Aphids choking the stems, the buds,
Crawling and sucking the sap,
A crystalline blanket smothering the bush.
And then—bathing them
In soapy dishwater every night.
And then—fulsome heads sprouting
Amid the thorns and black, white remains.
Can't believe they've had the pluck,
the luck to survive.
And now—these roses are a comfort!
We too have been infested,
Choked up on COVID-19.
And yet—encrusted blooms open into
Dazzling sunlight.

Mary Beth Lamb

I Heard the News

Today, oh—
Numbers climb, fall.
"Steady as she goes captain," but no...
Heart cries and a tear spills,
Mind twists and intestine clenches.

Today, reality rears its ugly head
        As sense of balance is skewed.
Swirling chaos rumbling in every cell
        The vortex whirls ever faster.
Breathe in; hold, breathe out;
Repeat.

Jan Radesky

A Pandemic Day

Paul has gone off for groceries
like a hunter in times of pandemic
armed with gloves and mask
I hope he doesn't catch anything
like the COVID 19 virus
but instead finds safe 6-foot encounters
on the senior waiting line
I pray for him to come safely home
As I am waiting for my zoom class to begin
I am waiting too for the pestilence to end
and the changed world to be revealed
that is already hinted at
As our CO_2 footprint goes down
and quiet descends
on our urban streets and highways
the voice of the turtle
can be heard in the land

Nina Serrano

Total U.S. deaths from COVID-19: 83,241

Rule-Followers

Long live the rule-followers.
We pass very carefully on the street,
physically distancing,
briefly making eye contact,
as small hands wave, signaling hello.
At nighttime the rules seem to change.
We pass, this time with little eye contact.
We physically distance, quickly passing.
At night we don't notice the walkers
who are smoking,
until after we've passed,
and we breathe and smell their smoke,
still hovering in the air
as we fill our lungs.
And we wonder,
Can the virus hitch a ride on the vapors?

Nancy Tolin

Masks On!

Masks on to the market,
masks on to the P.O. Box,
masks on to the bank—
We stand everywhere six feet apart
and look like Banditos y Banditas
holding up some train
behind the plastic barriers,
but we're only here looking
for when our out-of-stock TP arrives again!
A stranger approaches,
extends his elbow to me, it's not a High-5,
our hands aren't supposed to touch—
I elbow him back and laugh behind my mask,
it's local poet Bobby Richardson,
and we're both out doing our Friday
Coronavirus Pandemic tasks.
Masks on con mucho gusto,
mis Amigos y Amigas!

Peter Bray

Turn Down the Silence

Falling asleep on the couch;
   spouse and poodle snore in tandem;
While the clock ticks away
   on the kitchen wall;
Whooshes and hums from the dishwasher
   softly dance in rhythm
And float their way to the living room.
The clothes dryer rumbles and thumps
While the clothes washer creaks in a spin.
Air whistling through a vent in the floor,
Keeps me warm, as the furnace kicks in.
Outside the spring winds are howling,
But it's mostly quiet within.
Gone are the boisterous sounds,
Of two little girls.
No toys, no squabbles, no video games,
No exuberant din. Within.
Yet, the silence is so much louder now,
Than the clank and clamor ever was.
Back then.

Bud Light

Total U.S. deaths from COVID-19: 87,586

23

Friday, May 15, 2020
Keeping our distance

A Frightening World

This virus is frightening and so scary
It affects everyone,
even my deceased friend Harry.
We are hoarding everything
for almost a year later.
Canned and packaged foods
and all the toilet paper.
They have finally gotten smart
And starting to do their part.
Giving out things one at a time
Even if they only cost a dime.
The shelves are empty and pretty stark
Try to go shopping and no place to park.
Standing in lines that are almost
150 people or more.
Takes almost an hour to get to the door
Having to wipe everything off before
you prepare to eat
You can't even go places to meet.
Your friends are at home
and alone by themselves
Trying to find something on their shelves
Being alone and no place to go
It's lonely and makes the day go too slow.
I can think of things to do
Because I am sad and feel so blue.
I talk and text my friends on my phone
But it's not the same, I am still alone.
I do take walks to get fresh air
But stay my distance and
cover my face and hair.
I say hello
by waving my hand
But wish I was lying on a beach
in the warm sand.
Back home again and all alone
Going back and forth like a rolling stone.
I hope this virus ends so very soon

If not, I may be the first woman
to live on the moon.

Cooky Longo

Escape / Two Canoes

Escape, I do, Tuesday afternoon.
The sky is majesty in royal blue.
I see a guy drive by with two canoes
on top of his car. I want one, too!

I'd chart a course to a world that's new,
if only, if only I had a canoe.
But I have two feet and I'm wearing shoes,
so I venture forth to enjoy the view.

I'm mindful, ever mindful, to keep a distance,
aware that invisible threats float on air.
I straddle the path's edge
with cautious persistence,
granting fearful passersby six feet to spare.

Imposed isolation
goes against human nature,
but pandemic paranoia has even atheists
saying prayers.

When I have to pee the line is drawn.
Public restrooms make me scared.
My bladder full of coffee
wants to empty on the lawn,
so I cruise back home
to use the bathroom there.

Ramona Lappier

> *Total U.S. deaths from COVID-19: 91,023*

Day 47

We wake an arm's length apart
Inner smiles radiate
A brand new old couple
Sparking hope
Just in time

We contemplate what to let in
Yesterday's mail
Strategic grocery orders
Friends in virtual boxes
That's all

So we climb the stairs to a pale sunset
Cook as if company is coming
Splashes of red mingle with savory bites
With spicy sweet words for dessert

Scraping caked mapo ragu
  from the edges of the skillet
We decide to read before bed
But we keep talking
Diving to the place where fear is buried
Excavating truth
Just in time

Kathleen Herrmann

Between Friends

To say that one has never done
  anything wrong...
May be to suggest that one has never done
  ANYTHING
To speak of.
So bear with me, my friend
In my attempts to grow.
Because...if change is constant...

Then perfection could not possibly last
More than a moment.

Bud Light

Our World

Those with bare cupboards/
those without cupboards
Find common ground, hunger

Those with uncertain immunity/
those without immunity
Find common ground, six feet apart

Those who succumb in hospitals/
those who succumb on deserted streets
Find common ground, six feet under

Masked humanity asks

How did we get here?
When will it end?
What will it look like
on the other side?

A wolf "cries to the blue corn moon."

Mary Harrell

Total U.S. deaths from COVID-19: 93,103

Wednesday, May 20, 2020
New normal

Corona Haiku

Javier Bardem
In "No Country for Old Men"
Corona haircut

Pork chop for breakfast
Cheerios and Oreos
Corona diet

No bath yesterday
Or day before day before
Corona hygiene

Zoom conversations
Brave New World: What'sApp Facetime?
Corona, my Dear

Carolyn Plath

The Plague

The virus now surrounds us.
It haunts us and it hounds us.
It causes social distance
  and lowers our resistance.
The toilet paper blues
  comprise our latest news.
We notice upon entry,
  the market shelves are empty.
We wave instead of hugging.
Downhill we keep on chugging.
So how will we survive this plague?
Vaccination information?
Negative and vague.
Ah, but turn the page and please engage.
Remember scarlet fever, polio and mumps?
Those diseases came in clumps.
We conquered them because we could.
We'll win again, that's understood.
So don't despair and give up hope.
And please don't sit around and mope.
Let's overcome our fear,

knowing a new day is near.
When it's time to rejoice, raise your voice.
We will beat this plague, that much is clear!

Shirley King

Quarantine Dreams

I'm in a crowd watching a parade.
I'm in a hotel where I've previously stayed.
I'm bottle-necked
  at the entrance to the county fair.
People. People everywhere,
  breathing the same air.
A passing stranger elbows me—
and doesn't give an apology.

My everyday life of the past
every night in my dreams is cast.
Perhaps a forecast of things to come.
Perhaps those times are forever done.
By the sun I shrug through
  my quarantine routines.
By the moon I slip into my quarantine
dreams.

Becky Bishop White

Total U.S. deaths from COVID-19: 97,249

What I Told Myself
Before the Zoom Reading

Stop crying for the dead.
Take a shower and wash your hair.
Stop crying for the sick.
Wear a shirt the color of lilacs.
Paint your face the color of a rose—
soft, pink, glowing.
Stop crying for your lost country—
practice smiling in the mirror.
Memorize your poems
so you can always look at the camera.
Drink a glass of wine to calm yourself—
realize it's impossible to stop the tears.
Apologize later.
Tell them you clicked on
"Join meeting," but you couldn't connect—
For a little while, stop crying.
Go count the falling stars,
instead of the deaths.

Johanna Ely

The Tide is Low

When I ventured out today, it was a gray
and overcast afternoon, the direct opposite
of the sunshine of yesterday. I thought to
myself, every day feels so different in this
season of governmental mandates,
unanticipated shortages, and shelter in
place orders.

I expected empty streets, sidewalks, parks,
signs banning parking in places where
people used to gather by the waterfront,
and such.

But what I see and feel goes deep as I walk.
Heading into the promenade, I notice that
the tide is out quite far. Having taken so

many pictures of The Red Baron, a town
landmark, in different lighting conditions, it
doesn't fully register that the front end of
the boat is nearly aground. Rather, my eyes
are riveted on the churning ridges of white
caused by ragged currents just past the
waterline. The swirling curves draw me into
them.

By the time I get to the pier, an
uncomfortable heaviness is creeping into
my bones. It's far too dark for three o'clock
in the afternoon. I pass through an opening
in the walkway by a bold "PARKING LOT
CLOSED DURING THE PANDEMIC" sign, and
yellow police tape cordoning off the parking
lot. Suddenly, I am lost, no one in sight in
any direction. Hurrying to the end of the
pier, I scan the shoreline like a seagull
gliding overhead, looking for some juicy
morsel. Some hope. I see things I never
noticed before, too much black mud, dead
plants, sticks and rocks covered by sludge in
the vast gap between shore and water.

I sit down on a bench and my head drops into
my waiting hands. I can't help thinking that
even the water is afraid to come close; is it
practicing safe distancing? It seems confused,
and leery of the shore, maybe of me.

Today the tide is lower than I have ever
seen it. I am paralyzed by the desolation. I
wonder if the tide can go any lower.

Beth Grimm

Total U.S. deaths from COVID-19: 99,673

27

Yellow Roses
Deny Nothing...

This morning, a drizzling mist meets me
at the doorway.
Though my body doesn't recoil,
the moisture doesn't draw aside either.

Bared skin feels fresh coolness,
while that beneath
the jacket quickly discerns humidity.

Sunday's naturally quiet streets
are so flavored
with the taste of continuing quarantine,
even the crows
can't feign enthusiasm.

Still, along the neighbor's fence, yellow roses
gently scent collecting rain drops.

Jerry Bolick

This Spring

The late rain prods
the white pear flowers
to waft away too early.

The hummingbird's voice,
a fierce clicking—
morse code, a warning.

Purple lavender,
abundant—
more pungent than pleasant.

Isolated lovers,
lie down to sleep,
curl into a question mark.

World-wide,
Coronavirus deaths—
260,000 and rising.

Laurie Hailey

Relationships Should Have Medals

Those who have mastered successful
relationships ought to have medals.
Relationships are elusive.
Few have what it takes
to make it in the club.

I often prayed, yearning to obtain one that I
could be proud of. To learn its secret.
But some secrets aren't meant to be shared.
And if they are, I am green with envy.

I used to crave elusive men. It fascinated me
that they were always moving.
I longed to move too!

Now I am stagnant in body, but my mind is
moving. Making important to-do-lists just to
stay relevant with the times. Blocking
acquisitions of roles and instead learning to
create my own.

Because of COVID-19, successful relationships
are even more elusive.
I wish someone told me about the
stubborn chaos of marriage,
I probably wouldn't have changed my name.

Aqueila M. Lewis-Ross

Total U.S. deaths from COVID-19: 101,420

28

Keeping the Distance
with the Coronavirus

To the creepy guy,
in the grocery line;
Standing too close,
despite the Covid-one-nine.

It is not me that you scare,
And not just the fear of death;
I want to breathe fresh, clean air,
not smell your stale cigarette breath.

You claim the government,
 Did not act quick enough;
While you refuse to catch your sneeze,
Or cover your cough.

What you fail to understand,
About this demand;
It's not about new laws,
Infecting our land.

It isn't just about,
This Corona disease;
Nobody wants you standing so close,
Take a step back,
BACK OFF ME, PLEASE!

You refuse to wear a face shield,
or respect my space;
I want you to spin on your toes,
Conduct an about-face.

I do not care if your mask is
tough leather with frilly lace;
PEOPLE ARE DYING,
SO, JUST COVER YOUR FACE!

You proclaim, it's a free country,
That you're just living your life;
But, I'm telling you to back off,
You don't stand this close to your wife.

Keep your distance.
Mind the gap.
It is high time that you
GAVE A CRAP!

Joseph L. Wilder

Impersonal Acts
of Kindness

On the sidewalk I nod
to the unknown passerby
Whose flimsy powder blue mask
is no safeguard for
herself
But only for
anonymous me.
My mask veils my smile.

Mary Susan Gast

Total U.S. deaths from COVID-19: 104,154

iRobot Again

Beep! Beep!
Powering Up!
Powering Down!
Beep! Beep!

You're only allowed 6ft!
The command to practice social distancing.
You must shelter-in-place!
Because touching anything might be the end
of the race.

I risk it all to see my baby laugh and play
at the neighborhood park.
But even parks are banned.
So we peek behind the curtains to see
who's out.

We extroverts practice a new indoor sport
creating schedules to have a valid routine.
I watch her scatter her toys
over wooden floors.
And that's ok!

I wonder if God whispered to the birds
the secret.
What the world needs now?

I wasn't taught how to love from afar.
I wasn't taught how to love at all.
So I remain stuck in desire.
Longing to defy gravity.
Longing to do what must be done.

This closing in isn't good for all:
Those beaten black & blue.
Some babies need space to grow
away from the perps.
There isn't enough hand sanitizer, lotions,
and blushes to cover sin thrice removed.

And they can't call 911 cuz there's not
enough medical supplies to save us all.

Who can save us?
GOD PLEASE SAVE US!
WILL YOU SAVE US?

We are rotten!
We've ruined our world and she's dying!
The levees can't hold the tears anymore!

Let the enslaved be free!
Beep.
Beep.
Beep.........................

Aqueila M. Lewis-Ross

Thunder

As colliding air masses of
Transience and transcendence
Meet over steamy seas,
I attempt to count the seconds
Between lightning flash and thunderclap,
To gauge the distance between myself
And the storm of loss.

In these baffling days we live with loss,
With full knowledge that it is only by
Keeping distance
From one another,
  from one and beloved another,
That we will overturn the storm
And return
Into community.

Mary Susan Gast

Total U.S. deaths from COVID-19: 106,421

Going Viral

In this time of virus the news and
The places I search for my muse
Vie for attention

Attention is a ragged thing
Torn by fear and disgust
For the time

I hear the sparring words
   of our sitting President
Pushing platitudes and racism
Pointing our attitudes toward despair

I cannot bear to
Leave my attention there
I turn to prayer

Read the Daily Office
Seeking breaths of fresh air
In a language long dead

That yet helps me to recall the anguish
Of recent plagues and plagues
Of centuries past

It is not the virus that haunts my thoughts
But the decay of democracy and decency
That makes me long to be free of America

To escape the pain I go
For a walk in the rain
Through the wetlands

By the Napa River
I maintain social distance from my neighbors
Converse with birds and watch

The
      River
            Flow by

Charles Kruger

Lord Give Us a Sign

Lord give us a sign
A sign that change is gon' come
A sign of hope, peace and love
A sign that cancels hate
That makes more than just America great
A sign that justice
   for Ahmaud, Breonna and George
Will not fade away
   like Oscar, Trayvon, Michael or Tamir
A sign that Black Lives Matter
   and blue ones aren't real
A sign that patriotism means wearing a mask
   and fighting for equality
Not condemning those that do
A sign that we are healing
A sign that we care
That we've learned from our mistakes and
   will do better for the future
A sign the spread is slowing
That we can vote by mail
A sign we are still America
And will live to tell the tale
A sign to help folks realize
   this isn't fake news
One that brings us together
   despite our views
Lord give us a sign this will come to an end
For more than ourselves we must fend
Lord give us a sign

Galen Kusic

Total U.S. deaths from COVID-19: 108,107

COVID-19 School Primer

A lways anxious
B racing myself for the worst
C aught in repetitive thoughts
D istancing from my usual supports
E yeing surfaces suspiciously
F raught with worries about unseen danger.
G rimly going to food stores
H oping to find a necessity
I n an aisle of empty shelves.
J udging my ability to cope while
K eeping up my spirits
L imiting my television exposure
M aking the best of free time
N oticing projects left undone
O ver the previous months
P romising to follow through while
Q uestioning my priorities.
R ealizing some unused abilities
S atisfying some previously ignored needs
T iming myself on boring tasks
U nderstanding and forgiving my limitations.
V arying my creative endeavors
W earing my feel-good clothes
X ercising my body and my mind
Y earning for normalcy while waiting for my
Z eal for life to be reborn.

Katrina Monroe

The Choice

We are, all of us,
Wholly unto ourselves,
Existing, as a thread,
Somewhere between
Nothingness and eternity
The choice, as to the weaving

Of the thread, and its coloring
Is OURS.

Bud Light

Benched
(For the anonymous guy in the picture)

What goes through his mind
as he stares at the strait
from a wooden bench
long enough for several others
to join him—although not now
during these coronavirus days
of social distancing.

Perhaps he's taking time away
from a house full of those he loves
but has had enough of for now.
Maybe he's wishing for something
he can't identify or is acutely grateful
for his luck at not catching the virus
and knowing no one who has.
Does he think normal will ever return,
that this bench will again hold friends?

Sherry Sheehan

Total U.S. deaths from COVID-19: 110,861

Friday, June 5, 2020
Not sightless among miracles

These are the Heroes

The horns are sounding from the marina,
  it must be 7 o'clock.
Blaring tribute to the first responders
  valiantly battling the pandemic,
Its tentacles wrapping 'round the globe,
  sucking life out of helpless victims,
Gasping and fearful, infected by the scourge.

Doctors, nurses, medical professionals
  save lives even when,
Masks and gloves to minimally protect them,
  are nonexistent.
We try to support them by practicing
  safe distancing and shelter in place,
But there are others at risk
  doing their work,
  unheralded for their contributions.

These are heroes too, their work essential
  in caring for the sick.
EMTs, ambulance drivers,
  pharmacists, postal workers.
Those who maintain the equipment
  essential for saving lives,
Housekeeping staff prove cleanliness
  conquers entanglement in the viral net.

Dedicated public health and social workers
  visit their clients,
The elderly, mentally ill
  and physically disabled,
Medical professionals willing to fly
  far from home
Some willing to go from Atlanta
  to help in New York.

These are the heroes,
  compassionate and kind,
Such is the essence of humanity at its best,
What we discover lies within each one of us,

Urging us forward;
  it all begins and ends
  with human kindness, with love.

Carol Gieg

A Sabbath Prayer

Days pass and the years vanish
  and we walk sightless among miracles.
God, fill our eyes with seeing
  and our minds with knowing.
Let there be moments when Your Presence,
  like lightning,
  illumines the darkness in which we walk.
Help us to see, wherever we gaze,
  that the bush burns, unconsumed.
And we, clay touched by God,
  will reach out for holiness
  and exclaim in wonder,
"How filled with awe is this place
  and we did not know it."

Central Conference of American Rabbis

Total U.S. deaths from COVID-19: 112,745

Sunday, June 7, 2020
Lament and remedy

Whose Shelter?
Which Virus?—A Lament

Immersed in tension-filled news
reports all morning, all so reminiscent,

I head down to the garden
after lunch,

for light spring pruning

of branches stricken with curl,

a sheltered privilege indeed—would
that it would be so easy

to cull the poisonous roots,
but the tree still stands.

Even for those of us not on the streets,
shelter has lost all its luster.

Jerry Bolick

White Privilege

It comes to us white people
before we are born
like an unsolicited credit card
that somehow
we can't revoke.
No matter whether we have been granted
the full credit limit,
No matter whether we have worked
to dislodge the stone of bigotry
and melt the ice of indifference,
Overlapping systems of oppression
give us an edge,
in surviving COVID-19,
in surviving, period,
free from the stalking terror
of 401 years of ingrained swaggering impunity

that screams with brandished weapons
and whispers,
in the awful intimacy of a chokehold
or the nonchalance of a knee
bearing down on a neck,
"Only white lives matter."

Time for white folks to drop the limp rancid veil
Of unholy innocence,
And go all human.

Mary Susan Gast

Cures

She consults her Book of Cures
only to find academia. USELESS!
Nothing that will work
on a nation brainwashed to cowardice.

Not giving up, she calls on
the ghosts of infinity.
The trick is to incant in retro.
The spirits gather at her feet,
make marks in the sand,
leave her to meditation and rumination
and return to other worlds.

She reads the marks in the sand,
lays her body over the strange words,
closes her mind and waits.

She awaits enlightenment.
When it comes she will
ingest and digest remedies.
She will share with the world.
Together the frightened darkness
will return to the light
and she will write the remedy
in the Book of Cures.

Jeannette DesBoine

Total U.S. deaths from COVID-19: 113,888

34

Metanoia

A world folding in on itself
selecting some to die
others to survive in self-isolation.

An enemy too small to see
on a planet too small to contain it
each person caught
in a familiar but alien environment
in a prison of their own thoughts
their routine disrupted
assumptions destroyed
expectations exploded
forced to re-evaluate all.

From simple behaviors to life choices
all is displayed
on a cold steel laboratory table
inspected and dissected
under the bright light of cultural change.

Some will relapse to the old ways
when the crisis is over
while others will be baptized
in the water of spiritual conversion
never to return to business as usual
turning their eyes toward personal change
and a vision of a possible new world order.

Katrina Monroe

At Home

Walking around
Meaningless,
One foot, then another.
Like decisions these acts are.
Wasting time in a time of
Precious time.
One foot, one decision, one time
Now.

Jan Radesky

Nonsense

Hopelessness makes sense.
Dreadful horrific sense.
Yet smack in its face
We glory at the uprising
Of hope beaten down
So many times that
Hope itself is senseless.
Senseless incorrigible hope.

Mary Susan Gast

Total U.S. deaths from COVID-19: 116,183

Sunday

It's only Sunday. No different than
any other day...or night.
Time stands still.
Holding its breath.
Turning blue, purple, and grey.
Gasping for air.
Gagging on designer vermin.
Choking on close proximity.

What day is it again???

Jeannette DesBoine

A COVID-19 Journal Entry

Sunday morning, April 26th. I am enjoying
the light outside my window. There is a
young avocado tree in the neighbor's yard
whose small leaves are a lovely greenish-
yellow and flutter in the very slight breeze.
Past that is a segment of a redwood. I can
see its trunk right up to the first few
branches before it is blocked by my window
shade. The sky is visible only in patches,
through the redwood branches.

The pressure of shelter-in-place is
increasing my capacity for contemplation so
that the leaf of an avocado tree might easily
be the day's most exciting encounter.

I reflect on the day's plans: a couple of
walks around the block, perhaps a brief
ZOOM meeting with some cousins, a movie
on TV. For days (weeks?) now, I've spent
hours (eight or nine) just sitting at my desk
staring at my computer, surfing the
internet. Mostly on Facebook. It is not much
of a life, really,
and I'm thinking I'd like to exercise some
discipline and get away from the computer,
but that frightens me. What will I be if I do
nothing? I consider whether I might spend

the entire day walking outside. I never
thought such a thing was possible unless I
were "going for a hike." But why not just
walk?

With no work, no income, no expectations
and no demands, the possibilities to lean and
loaf are legion.

Imagine that.

And by way of a footnote and learning
something new every day: If you google the
phrase "lean and loaf" you will get
numerous references to lean meatloaf
before you'll stumble upon Walt Whitman.

Onward.

Charles Kruger

Pandemic Memories

Today was a good day
To Hear and See
To Breathe and be
To Love, and feel Thanks
To Be Alive.
And to also think of those,
So near and dear, so many
Who aren't.

Bud Light

Total U.S. deaths from COVID-19: 118,928

Waiting

The pandemic
is endemic
I sit with
pen in hand
my ink runs dry

I stand
and sanitize
list-make
wash hands again
scrub every room

I search for signs
in the sky
see holes
in the ozone
the clouds
layered
with potholes

I swerve to avoid
the ER
physically distant faces
reeking of fear
On the next corner
arms raised high
angry eyes glaring
above bandanas

My hands are bound
keyboard silenced
waiting for vaccine
waiting for peace
waiting to breathe

Deborah Grossman

At the Dollar Store

Yesterday, at the Dollar Store
I bought too much
for a single trip to the car.
The cart not allowed
out of the store,
jammed up against the door,
I juggled several bags,
some stakes for the garden,
a gallon bottle of bleach.
Not enough arms. When a Black woman and
her teenage daughter approached.
We can help, the mother said.
The daughter hefted two clumsy bags
and carried them to the rear of my car.
An old White woman, at the dollar store,
accepting a random act of kindness.
And that was exactly what I needed
to get me through the day.

Louise Moises

Total U.S. deaths from COVID-19: 120,867

Friday, June 19, 2020
Juneteenth

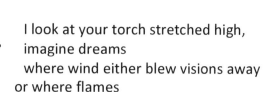

Monumental Rights

Glimmer of ghosts whose
hopeful hearts and hands
like wings flew to catch
the American Dream, a chance
for inclusiveness. Your copper oxidizes
to green yet
stone base unwavering to weather,
strong and steady,

a captain as turbulent
river and ocean are met
with exuberance, you guide yearnings
so chances

can stay afloat. My eyes feast
between prayer and awe.
Courage is a map
where roadblocks are not shown,

shadows of former strife cast not hardship,
but light of toil.
Does your robe drape
this undocumented fear?

I am reminded that the past existed,
that the present
instantly becomes the past,
and yet you've seen

then and now many stares starving for faith,
you've seen wounds seep into cracks,
scabs like hollow rawness

reopen and heal into scars,
scars that thicken skin
but never suture
the unpinned fight for liberty.

I look at your torch stretched high,
imagine dreams
where wind either blew visions away
or where flames

gathered heat and quests burned
longer, brighter
where equality is standard
and opportunity is real

Suzanne Bruce

from Let America be America Again

Let America be the dream the dreamers
        dreamed—
Let it be that great strong land of love
Where never kings connive nor tyrants
        scheme
That any soul be crushed by one above.

(It never was America to me.)

Langston Hughes, 1935

> *Total U.S. deaths from COVID-19: 122,196*

Hubris

What made us think we'd be immune?
Didn't we read about
the honey bee hive collapse?
Didn't we follow the progress
of white nose in bats?
Didn't we understand
about the effect of pollution on the fish?
Why are we so slow to connect the dots?
Did we think we'd solved biology:
tamed the jungle, flattened volcanos,
destroyed fungus,
held at bay the floods with aging dams?
Where were you
during the fires last summer?
How many hurricanes
are predicted for this year?
What happened to a short tornado season?
Maybe we forgot to read the fine print.
Maybe whistling in the dark can work.
Maybe we don't need
a sense of history and its lessons.
Maybe we just can't get it together.

But let's wake up to reality.
Just once, just now.
Of course, you say
reality is ever changing
within our closed system.
But
let's face what we are. Let's face our folly,
our hubris.
We're just one of the endangered animals on
this glorious planet
that isn't designed for our pleasure, safety
or exclusive benefit.
That's a basic rule. It's best to understand it.

Ronna Leon

Benediction

May God bless you with discomfort,
At easy answers, half-truths,
And superficial relationships
So that you may live
Deep within your heart.

May God bless you with anger
At injustice, oppression,
And exploitation of people,
So that you may work for
Justice, freedom and peace.

May God bless you with tears,
To shed for those who suffer pain,
Rejection, hunger and war,
So that you may reach out your hand
To comfort them and
To turn their pain to joy

And may God bless you
With enough foolishness
To believe that you can
Make a difference in the world,
So that you can do
What others claim cannot be done
To bring justice and kindness
To all our children, all in need.
Amen.

A Franciscan blessing

Total U.S. deaths from COVID-19: 123,084

Wednesday, June 24, 2020
Will we remember?

Fragments of Memory

What sound most reminds you
of your childhood?
My mind sifts through fragments of memory

The jingle of the ice cream truck
The rain bird sprinkler rhythmically swishing
while watering the lawn
on a hot summer day
The tinny sound of my transistor radio
in its leather case

Lazy, long-forgotten sounds—
those nostalgic, comforting sounds
of childhood

The memory of fishing at the lake,
my trusty transistor radio
behind me on the steep, rocky embankment,
and casting, bringing that pole
back up over my head,
while (unbeknownst to me) the hook catches
the leather strap of my radio,
and then with a forward throwing motion,
I feel the unexpected tug
as I expertly release the line
and watch with dismay and horror
as my radio goes sailing through the air
and splashes into the lake's serene water

The day the music stopped

The day life as we know it stopped

What sound most reminds you
of your childhood?
How will children remember
these days of sheltering in place?
Stripped of social freedoms,
masked, confused, crazy-bored,

while the economy tanks
and their parents fret

Just how will children remember
the day life as we know it stopped

Nancy Tolin

Masked

Benched man
replaced by masked
woman standing

for liberty,
coronavirus-like
spikes in her crown,

newly confined
by garb required
against the pandemic.

Do you remember
her nose and mouth,
how beautiful they looked

welcoming all
who yearned
to breathe free?

Sherry Sheehan

Total U.S. deaths from COVID-19: 124,992

40

Black Willow

This year the earth is closer to truth
        And terror; menacing Lord,
He's there in the detail of each flower,

Spring garden vine choked little bruise
        On the land, dead hearted;
Empty, no stream of morning traffic

Clouds paddle on the splattered wall
    Cattle move through open
 meadow, snow slumps from pine

 and the black willow; Faint metallic
        taste of fear, how people
change, drift away, die, those whose

humor enjoyed, childish jokes,
        anecdotes simple sweetness
of thy neighbors, ordinary friends.

 Now they are merely candles hidden
        by dust while in the day's
 disorder, fat flicker of the pileated

woodpecker, pagan priest smart hard
        hearted; everywhere you look
 is this language of passing, of pestilence,

 the inner angel of rage confronts private
        breathing that try the lungs
collapsing under the grey ventilators,

green rubber gloves their fluency, sea blue
        masks that eclipse the mouth,
the nose while cherry trees
in the nearby park

glisten instructing: find beauty's brother
now shuddering, prophetically
        a gilt gift at the brink of Bosch's hell.

Leonore Wilson

Safe Breathing on Juneteenth

The social fabric is in turmoil
and needs some serious mending.
I bend over my still singing treadle
and assemble a few more face masks
for my daughter, the hospice nurse,
and her airline pilot hubby,
cute ones for the grandkids,
and another for a friend.

While thousands are dying from Covid-19,
brave souls around the globe are protesting
the senseless murder of Black people.
My heart is with you, my brethren,
demonstrating in every state
plus D.C. where I grew up.
This Juneteenth I march with you in spirit
as I sit down to sew these silly masks.

George Floyd, Breonna Taylor,
Rayshard Brooks,
it's too late to sew masks for you.
But I fold and iron this cotton cloth
and stitch the seams to enable
a friend, a relative, a neighbor
to go outside and breathe
a little more safely tomorrow,
so we all can breathe easier.

Alyza Lee Salomon

Total U.S. deaths from COVID-19: 126,169

41

Sunday, June 28, 2020
The cautious and the rash

Reopening

1.
For months
that felt like years
I kept out of sight,
the virus whistling for me
to come out and play.

I hid in my home
behind locked doors—
no signs of life,
curtains pulled across
dark windows.

Spring came and blossomed.
Sweet rose, calla lily, daffodil.
I ached to blossom too.

2.
In the summer heat
of a late afternoon,
I walk downtown
past shops that once again
say OPEN,
a black mask stretched snugly
over my nose and mouth.

Sitting in the shade
of your backyard,
we look at each other
in amazement.
How long has it been?
Our hearts open
slowly, cautiously,
one petal at a time.

Johanna Ely

Young at Heart

I see them in the park
I see them in the street,
At the beach and on tv….

They whisper and shout
In joy and competition
And laugh and run
Like lambs…

To the slaughter.

COVID deny-ers
Or simply unaware,
They risk it all
For wholesome joy
And friendships born and blossoming
And witless,
Bring it home to mom.

And dad.

And gramma and gramps.

Young at heart,
And young at lung,
When life hangs balanced
On a COVID thread.

Roger Straw

Total U.S. deaths from COVID-19: 126,986

I Got a Hole in My Afro

I got a hole in my afro
It's not because I'm old,
I got a hole in my afro
Let the truth be told,
I got a hole in my afro
I took one to the head,
I got a hole in my afro
They pronounced me dead!

I dreamed of being a NBA star
I got a full ride; just to go far,
I wanted to live the good life..!
Have some children-just one wife,
NOT! He said my cellphone was a knife.
Now, my family must fight for my rights!
I wanted to be, All-I-can-be...
Maybe even join the Military!
But none of those things happen for me...
Because my heart stopped beating,
I then stopped breathing...
And this is after I start bleeding!

This is for all the Black men
That held-up their hands!
And for the other brother—found...
Sitting down on the ground,
He got shot 20 times...
Tell me...!
What was his crime?
Did he run a stop sign?
Can you FATHOM?
The terror he felt before they Blast-um!
He had a mother!
Was he a father?
Did he have sisters or brothers?
When he pled for his life,
Did he survive a wife?

I got a hole in my afro...
Where hair use to be!
I got a hole in my afro...
Dear mother now bury me!

Mary "Lady-D" Brown

The U.S. Is a Papadum

We took a bite of papadum
And saw the USA
We took a bite of papadum
So fragile to our dismay;
We felt it chip away
We took a bite of papadum
It crumbled before our eyes
The U.S. is a papadum
So called leaders feed us lies
Will there be more papadum?
Or just apple pie
Our nation is a papadum
Together we must rise
The people need more papadum
For equality let's strive
The final bite of papadum
We hope it's not the last
Democracy was a papadum
It's loudly breaking fast

Galen Kusic

When I Rise Up

When I rise up above the earth,
And look down on the things that fetter me,
I beat my wings upon the air,
Or tranquil lie,
Surge after surge of potent strength
Like incense comes to me
When I rise up above the earth
And look down upon the things that fetter me.

Georgia Douglas Johnson

> *Total U.S. deaths from COVID-19: 128,689*

You Want a Confederate Monument? My Body is a Confederate Monument

I have rape-colored skin. My light-brown-blackness is a living testament to the rules, the practices, the causes of the Old South.

If there are those who want to remember the legacy of the Confederacy, if they want monuments, well, then, my body is a monument. My skin is a monument.
[...]
I am a black, Southern woman, and of my immediate white male ancestors, all of them were rapists. My very existence is a relic of slavery and Jim Crow. [...]

Caroline Randall Williams
New York Times, June 26, 2020

From **The New York Times**. ©2020 The New York Times Company. All rights reserved. Used under license.

We'll Never Turn Back

Now we've been 'buked
 and we've been scorned
We been talked about sure as you' born
But we'll never turn back
        No we'll never turn back
        Until we walk in peace
        And we'll have equality
        And we'll have equality.

We have walked
through the shadows of death
We had to walk all by ourselves
        But we'll never turn back

No we'll never turn back
Until we walk in peace
And we'll have equality
And we'll have equality.

Anthem, Student Nonviolent Coordinating Committee

Uplifting

That big old **X** dominated the flag,
Crossed out the Confederacy's ties to
The Union, they said.
Nothing personal.

That big old **X**, in fact, obliterated
Freedom,
Hope,
Full humanity,
For the enslaved
and their descendants,
White-d out
Compassion,
Liberty and justice
For all.

As of this July 1st
That big old **X**
No longer sways
Over any state capitol.

With the crash of symbols in Mississippi,
May the star-bright spirits of
Medgar Evers, Fannie Lou Hamer,
Vernon Dahmer, Herbert Lee...
Stir the air ever more vividly
with their angel wings.

Mary Susan Gast

Total U.S. deaths from COVID-19: 130,071

The Return

They come when we're maybe
dabbling in verses—
homing coyotes on the roofs
of the City's Victorians,
and grizzlies and bison in Yellowstone,
their mighty war
drum hearts, and on provincial streets;
wild boars
roaming Italian towns, a long burst
of Japanese Sika deer
toddling the still streets of Nara,
and a family of Egyptian
geese like a future hung with trophies crossing
the empty tarmac of Tel Aviv; without humans
the life blood of fish, and rumored dolphins
now in the gleaming blue canals of Venice,
and overhead swans unassailable
and wild ducks
like a spur of elegists returning to the
cathedral fountains
of Florence and sanguine Rome,
nascent goats
browsing triumphantly in the clipped gardens
and hedges
and cantering along the lanes
of a Welsh seaside
town, and flocks of wild turkeys strutting
down Harvard Yard
as if remembering the forests that once grew
there;
territorial pigeons in the mother ground of
London too;
Our earth is healing, an unleavened healing
of borders
from the Pandemic's dirt veined waste,
an aftermath
of some new Eden, what is denied now
rightfully theirs,
emissaries of hope and possibilities not just
flesh and bone,

daring us to dream of a better world,
this tribulation gone forever.

Leonore Wilson

Summer Reminiscing

Summer is the age of orange-like maze,
Of red-slashed skies at sunset and at dawn,
that turn
To crimson fire, a golden haze, and quench
Its blaze in blue, when day is done.
An age of scarlet-flashing gypsy skirts;
A time of laughter, love and weeping;
Summer is a sun that flirts but once;
A luscious sweet, a fantasy
Not for the keeping.

But what of summers full of hopeful dreams
That contemplate our life and death
  and fears
(Realities which only youth can see).
And what of summers spent
By quiet, cool-shaded streams,
Where love loomed ripe and sweet
In those, our greenest years?

(Oh, Golden days, in times like these
Where can those summers be?)

Bud Light

Total U.S. deaths from COVID-19: 130,704

45

Anger

Anger, the bastard child
of that troubled union
before Reality left Expectations crying
on her bed
before Chaos abandoned Hope
alone in the street
before Frustration beat up Effort on the job
and Heartache conquered Humanity
at every turn.

Our daily lives co-opted by an enemy
too small to see
major sacrifices made not just for ourselves
but for the protection of us all
hoping together we could rebound.
Our progress wiped out
by selfishness and stupidity.

The nightmare of a brutal death
awakening us
from the dream of a just society
to the frustrating discovery of the untruths
laid before our unseeing eyes for decades.
Our blindness allowing for pain and injustice.

A sense of moral righteousness stoked
by the looting, burning and violence
in the street
so that even the peaceful are greeted by
heavy handed tactics befitting criminals.
An assault on our belief that lives are sacred.

Anger oozes from the cracks in the street,
the bars in the jail cells,
the tv screen showing a party or a protest
and our worn-out front stoops
from lingering too long,

until that anger settles in the heart
ready to boil over at any moment.

Katrina Monroe

What the Almighty Said
in the Garden of Eden

You know, I created it ALL good.
All the
Jangling,
Jarring,
Incongruent,
Elements of
Identity, trait, and spirit.

Tend the garden
   and keep the blessed contradictions,
Composted into
The wholeness and holiness
Of the earth
Where I have sown compassion
In the rich soil of variegation.

Let Me keep you from
   the grave and horrible perception
That humankind will be
Either or
Only
Evil or
Good.

Mary Susan Gast

Total U.S. deaths from COVID-19: 133,079

"Chang'e Thursday Inkan"

I woke up to sleep.
Fantail orange fanta.
How this has grown.
With so little water.
Tepid Henry.
Knew.

...Placing each hue.
Wingbeats in a vacuum.
Bluest of blues.
Plumage magnificat.
Sailing well past dawn.
Inkan chime seal.
Sleep to wake.
Wake to wake.
Chrysanthemum blooms.
Woken to sleep.

"Chang'e Friday Inkan"

I woke up to slumber.
Fantail yellow.
Orange fanta.
Swimming ballerina.
How this has grown.
With so little water.
Tepid Henry.
Knew.

...Roil upon me.
Scales of hue.
Upon this dock.
Docket.
Found you.
Deleterious.
Mossed deer.
Gleaming.
Platinum.
In the dew.

Tom Stanton

Quarantined Lover's Song

Maybe I should write a
Quarantined Lover's Song,
one that we can all sing or hum along.
Maybe something laid-back
like Leonard Cohen,
"Our Lady of the Harbor"
with "tea and oranges" again.
No, No, No, it has to stand on its own merit:
Naked oysters, lipstick, a winter's coat,
but don't wear it.

Sea foam, skybird, a gentle touch,
but where are you?
Teasing seduction, envelope,
feel all the colors,
wandering, wondering, then I found you!

Work on it, plow on it when you can—Corona-
Bologna, we need to feel alive again! Mask it!
Ask it, "Are we at 6-feet and OK?
I'll love you with an Elbow-bump today!"

Peter Bray

Total U.S. deaths from COVID-19: 134,907

What Bird Sings

Each morning from the thatch of treetops,
whose notes hit the open ground,
slab of tongue
where the children learned to walk

and run; what thrives here still
in the ministry
of laurels, oaks, madrones, whose morning
song melts down a candle flame then abruptly

starts again when the Herculean sun gives way
to dusk. Neither of us wants to know,
no one goes to the bookcase to find the field
guides,

hunts down the old binoculars,
neither wants to name,
for naming is possessing and isn't song enough
like an infant incubating, button fist a comfort,
sweet

jewel of lips...Bird in nature's pantry,
in the shirt
sleeves of a pandemic spring, bird adjusting
its vocabulary, with more challenge than
pride as quail

in the canyon dawn-sniff the watercress and
wring
their calls like steeple bells; oh bird whose
language
trickles dime-size, see our flesh fenced in like
barbed

wire...Cloistered soul, teach us devotion
again, little
fugitive to be your pupil in the floe of desire,

to be a privileged attendant, prodigious
husband, insatiable bride.

Leonore Wilson

COVID Lockdown

In El Dorado County there's a town
Where every night at 8
Dogs and humans step outside,
Raise their heads to the tree-framed sky,
And howl.

Then the relay of "good nights" commences,
Volleyed from yard to yard,
Evoking an emotional ambience
categorically closer to
"The Waltons" than
to prison.

Mary Susan Gast

Total U.S. deaths from COVID-19: 136,110

When I Was Whole

I would wake and
wait till it was light,
or often go out in the
starlit dark to grab my
paper. Coffee and paper:
the ritual was like warming
my hands over a fire: a start
to the day. Unlock the
back door for grandson,
make him toast and water for
school, out to the car, perfectly timed,
or not, to trudge with the army of
parents, our children to the doors.

When I was whole—
all of my parts still inside
me, not disposed of in medical
waste—periods never bothered me, I was glad
to have them, stopping
only for pregnancies.
Ticking in and out the years, the
decades, thirties, forties—
I thought that was the end
of the story of those organs.

I thought I'd be getting coffee
and paper day in and out, until
everything changed. They cut
out my insides and the world reeled
and stopped. Thousands of people are
dying from an invisible plague.

There is no more school, and
I am not whole, yet still alive.
The days of my organs
inside me are over, and what lies ahead
of me, and all of us, no one can say.

Lauren Coodley

To Grasp the Moment

Time is everything.
It never dies
It never lived
It is eternity.

It is limitless.
A silent pool, collecting
Drop after drop.

It is unendingness;
It never seems to have begun.

To those who look to times past, and future
Unknown to us
As we, perhaps,
Remain unknown to one another;
To those who seek the answers
To questions yet unasked
And always will.
Look hard. Time stands not still.

What matters is what we do with it.
All of us.

Bud Light

Total U.S. deaths from COVID-19: 138,457

Memorial Day: Pantoum for Twin Pandemics

Here at the tomb of the unknown citizen
one hundred thousand bodies lie
some arrive in refrigerated trucks
some imported from crematoria

one hundred thousand bodies lie
this pandemic sunders families
some imported from crematoria
electorates, races, and religions

this pandemic sunders families
no exceptions for the rich & famous
electorates, races, & religions
old and young, remember when

no exceptions for the rich & famous
is Corona the last scion of democracy
old and young, remember when
government cared about the people

is Corona the last scion of democracy
I said *bodies lie* but they never do
government cared about the people
I scan the obituaries

I said *bodies lie* but they never do
murdered by racism and inaction
I scan the obituaries
death by arrogance and greed

murdered by racism and inaction
what is the antonym for remorse
death by arrogance and greed
what is the antidote for laissez-faire

what is the antonym for remorse
here at the tomb of the unknown citizen
what is the antidote for laissez-faire
what is the remedy for *I really don't care?*

Sandra Anfang

At a Time Like This

At a time like this, scorching irony, not
convincing argument, is needed. O! had I the
ability, and could I reach the nation's ear, I
would, today, pour out a fiery stream of biting
ridicule, blasting reproach, withering sarcasm,
and stern rebuke.

Frederick Douglass, 1852

Memorial Day Pantoum Rebuts Itself

I said *democracy* but my words lie
on soft couches beside stocked pantries
democracy's a racist with identity disorder
Corona memorizes each address

on soft couches beside stocked pantries
Corona feeds its fury
memorizes each address
in the Navajo Nation & homeless camp

Corona feeds its fury
in Detroit, Chicago & the barrio
in the Navajo nation & homeless camp
but they dub it an equal opportunity disease

in Detroit, Chicago & the barrio
the poor fill makeshift clinics
but they dub it an equal opportunity disease
while the tyrant tweets contempt

the poor fill makeshift clinics
I said *democracy* but my words lie
while the tyrant tweets contempt
democracy's a racist with identity disorder.

Sandra Anfang

Total U.S. deaths from COVID-19: 140,346

50

Long Time No See:
Poets in the Moment

Welcoming her
I cannot see her glorious smile under the mask
her uncut hair hangs longer
We catch up
She'd written a new book of poems
Bravo!
Gone through the pandemic rollercoaster
Me too!
We sit in the back yard shade
drinking in the moment
the right now of it
among hummingbirds finches
and a swaying windchime in the warm breeze
The moment relaxes and stretches
to read each other our poems
Some uplift Some face the plague
and climatic traumas
Then we write new poems
in a complicated form
though we are both usually free versers
letting the poem take us where it may
Remembering how we used to sing in her car
on the way to and from live poetry readings
We sing the old favorites
The finches sing too. Our duet has a choir
Raising goosebumps on my arms
She leaves promising to return
The songs hang in the air
In the early evening I go to water the yard
The plants sing out:
"It's the hammer of justice
It's the bell of freedom
It's the love between
my brothers and my sisters
all all all over this land."

Nina Serrano

Maybe Today

I haven't cried yet.
About the coronavirus,
And the fears and limitations,
And death and loss,
And the glowering menace
On the horizon
That might be
The ash of lives and woodlands,
But could just as easily be
The existential omen
For humanity henceforth and forever shrouded
In pandemic.

I haven't cried yet.
But yesterday I saw a white butterfly
In mercurial dance mode
Above the sidewalk
My grandson and I once walked
To and from his grade school,
When his friends would join us
Babbling and running,
When the sky glinted blue with sunlight,
And dragonflies escorted us into magic realms.

I haven't cried yet.

But today may be the day.

Mary Susan Gast

Total U.S. deaths from COVID-19: 141,682

Say Their Names

We march from distant points
at opposite ends of town
converge on the fairgrounds

three miles separate us
though it might as well
be a continent

we have no barrio to speak of
but it's no secret that the east side
is the bedroom of the working classes.

Side by side with twenty-somethings
we punctuate
the air with fists and signs

say their names
say their names
say their names

While dopplered car horns answer
a man emerges from a sunroof
flares a Mexican flag like a giant kite

his face a dueling ground
of joy and tears
the horns continue their applause

say their names
say their names
say their names

At the fairgrounds
we learn what it takes
to understand a people's pain

the ways to offer
service and respect to sisters
black & brown—

what books to read
which films to watch

a syllabus in getting woke.
Before we disperse
we take a knee
a simple act
humbling & quaint
as if to propose to the world
in all its rainbow beauty.

Will you take me
as I am
for better & for worse?

say their names
say their names
say their names

Sandra Anfang

On Solidarity

Solidarity is not a matter of agreeing with,
of supporting, liking, or being inspired by
the cause of a group of people. Though all
of these might be part of solidarity,
solidarity goes beyond all of them.
Solidarity has to do with understanding the
interconnections that exist between
oppression and privilege, between the rich
and the poor, the oppressed and the
oppressors.

Ada Maria Isasi-Diaz
from "Mujerista Theology"

Total U.S. deaths from COVID-19: 144,569

Six Miles Away

On Tuesday mornings,
I drove the six miles to your school
Its faded facade looking weary
from decades of trying
You would fly to the back table
Where we conspired
to hack the printed code
"Run, run as fast as you can.
You can't catch me,
I'm the gingerbread man."

It was late December
when your childhood ended
Dad overdosed and died
Mom went to jail
Grandma brought you to school,
when she wasn't too high

Primal screams and chair throwing
Frightened classmates shrank away
Exiled to the principal's office—again

On your small shoulders,
you bear the misery
Of ancestors you don't even know
Still, you burned through
word games and tongue twisters
Beaming when you got it right.

On Tuesday afternoons,
I drove the six miles home
Skirting drab concrete buildings,
brown weedy lawns,
iron gated doors, run-down bars
I-80 depositing me
onto more familiar terrain
Winding down to the waterfront
past groomed yards

Pulling into my driveway,
blushes of bougainvillea
framing the front door

Six miles away, you send your SOS
It rises, joining a chorus of innocent pleas
No more pretending
I hear you

Kathleen Herrmann

Riff on Psalm 126

Torn with tears,
Rent with sorrow,
Nonetheless
We plant,
For tomorrows
Yet unconceived,
By us,
Anyway.

Mary Susan Gast, from *Conspiracy of Hope*

Reminder

When you see something that is not right,
not fair, not just, you have to speak up.
You have to say something;
you have to do something.

John Lewis at Trump Impeachment Trial 2020

Total U.S. deaths from COVID-19: 146,764

It's Sunday

It's Sunday ... if you care.
And even if you don't care...
It's Sunday.

Shall we stop and breathe...
Shall we bend in prayer...
Or shall we dig fresh bullets from the backs of
our futures?

Choices are afforded us by nature of the day
of the week.
Sunday is a holy day. A day we look to
religion to solve our problems...To bring us
peace...To answer our prayers...

But our knees no longer bend.
Not because of us...
But because of policy!

It's Sunday...
A day of reflection...
The day of counting our corpses...
A day of burying our dead.

Sunday...

It's Sunday...

It's always Sunday in Black America.

Jeannette DesBoine

July 4th, 2020

America, your people are falling
through the cracks.
With every vote, demonstration,
and molten statue
they cry out for you to change your violent ways.

America, the foundations upon which you stand
are cracked until you deal with the mold and rot
of hatred, murder, and oppression you have dealt.

America, I await the day those ideals you taught
begin to mold the true reality of everyone's lives
for your hymns touting liberty and justice for all
are merely myths crackling like dust in the wind
that bury the truth of centuries of sorrow and pain.

If my brothers and sisters cannot breathe freely,
then how dare we call this a land of liberty?
If money is the rubric that divides our people,
then how dare we claim that all people are equal?
If my neighbors are sleeping out on the streets,
then how dare we say this is a land of welcoming?

America, put down your hot dogs, beer,
and fireworks.
This is no time to celebrate. This is the time to
end hate.

D.L. Lang

Total U.S. deaths from COVID-19: 148,213

54

Crossing Over

The Edmund Pettus Bridge
Spans the Alabama River,
Spans the flow of history.

In 1965 marchers crossing that bridge,
Heading from Selma to Montgomery,
Paused at the apex to see what lay ahead.

They went forward, eyes open
Into the blockade of helmeted,
baton-wielding, tear-gassing,
agents of the status-quo repression.

They went forward, arms linked, hearts open,
Heads cracked open, ribs splintered,
Bones brutally fractured,
Into the fray that was weaving a new era
From the shambles of the past,
Stalwart, good-trouble-making John Lewis
In the vanguard.

Today the Edmund Pettus Bridge
Spanned the Jordan River
As it spanned the flow of history.

The funeral procession crossing that bridge,
John Lewis' body heading from Selma to
  (be welcomed and to lie in state
   at the Capitol in)
Montgomery,
Paused, with reverence, at the apex
to see what lay ahead.

They went forward, eyes open,
Over the red rose petals gracing the pavement
In commemoration of the bloodshed in the
Fight for freedom.

The spirit of John Lewis went forward, heart open,

 And surely he saw
    A band of angels comin' after me,
The spirit of John Lewis went forward, heart open,
And surely he saw,
     A band of angels comin' after me
     Comin for to carry me home.

Where, from his new vantage point,
He will persist in roiling our national
conscience
With his hope-laden, love-giving, joy-inducing
  courage-strengthening
"Good Trouble," his benediction.

Mary Susan Gast, July 26, 2020

Help Redeem
the Soul of America

Walking proud
For purpose
For freedom
He risked his life on call
Day in and day out
For a cause he was willing to die for
His message was clear
It never wavered
Inspired by a love for all
He was unbreakable
He made good trouble
He reminded us who we truly are
Never forget
The man that marched
And risked it all
For us to be free

Galen Kusic

> *Total U.S. deaths from COVID-19: 152,115*

All the Pain and Glory

I never did
which is to say
among other things
it's unfathomable
and by that I mean
tell me
tell me what you can
you can't say too much
which is only to say
show me
what living's like
multi-generation
the cellular embedments
which can, must, will

and since we're talking today
let me stop here to say these matters
are uncomfortable
but I am not fragile and it can't
be turned away from
so now let's eye to eye
and by that I mean only
tell me
tell me all of it
which is to say
I want to see you
to see you
to see
to finally
finally
see.

Shawna L. Swetech

Lady Liberty

Made of steel and copper,
she stands strong,

not a candidate for toppling,
because of slave-owning,

instead a piece of history
we revere,

built in Paris, a gift from France,
shipped to us in 1885,

long may she inspire the best
our nation has to offer.

Sherry Sheehan

I Dream a World

I dream a world where all
Will know sweet freedom's way,
Where greed no longer saps the soul
Nor avarice blights our day.
A world I dream where black or white,
Whatever race you be,
Will share the bounties of the earth
And every man is free....

Langston Hughes, 1926

Total U.S. deaths from COVID-19: 154,575

everything changes

in an instant
everything changes—
our bodies may become
the battlefield

in this aggressive COVID fight;
how skillfully the virus navigates
at the molecular level—
in contrast, we humans falter
at the basic cell, organ and
organ system levels;
then in desperation, at the human level,
we pray for a vaccine—
an effective vaccine to share with humanity

now the battlefield shifts
from coronavirus outbreak
to economic upheaval,
perhaps leading to financial despair
and psyches
stressed nearly beyond resiliency

again, defiantly, the battlefield shifts
from protests and racial strife sparked
by a senseless killing,
to the exposed inequities
that impact the marginalized people
of this world—
Black Lives Matter—we humans falter again,
but this time our white silence weeps

the battlefield
our bodies may become
everything changes—
in an instant

Nancy Tolin

I'd Rather Be on a Zooming Train Than a Zoom-Train

Cho cho,
…….choo Choo,
choo, chew…choo!
Round da bend sound,
foggy dog.
Railroad
2d
low-fi
squawk trak'!
Track,

… Better fall lightly.
In the night….

Dan flatly alright…!
Acrid smoke in zoom moon screen.
Can be fatal.
Perform, Bhutan Butoh, Bhutoh.
Silent bird dance,
on rectangle,
tangle.
Tangle dis
dis:
this,

entangled.
mizen twiss, lwis.

Tom Stanton

Total U.S. deaths from COVID-19: 156,098

Piccolo Orso*

*Italian: Little Bear

The front window-sills of houses
In Noe Valley,
San Francisco's
High-end suburb on the hill
Above the Mission,
Are galleries for
Placards these days.

Held fast to pane glass with Scotch Tape
Are tack-board admonishments
To neighbours unnerved by
The continued march of Corona,
Bearing words that soothe:

EVERYTHING WILL BE OK.
WE WILL SURVIVE.
WE WILL GET THROUGH THIS.

And then, Mister
Teddy Bear makes his appearance.

Stuffed wool, thread and varnished button eyes
Comprises our friend's being.
Little Teddy sits
In the window-sill of a house
Soaking up the morning sun,
Just chilling, passing small
Children on Jersey Street
Enjoy his cute, adorable,
Calming presence. Tiny fingers point up
at their find:

Little Teddy
Kicking it, calm and lounging
Next to a hand-drawn
Placard, reminding block residents
What Hunter's Point, Sunnydale,
Seminary, Eastmont and I
Have always known to be fact:

BLACK LIVES MATTER.

A child's bed-time companion

Moved on up
To the front of the house.
He's on constant display
Like a hard-plastic preening
Mannequin in Neiman Marcus'
Store-front window,

There in the window-sill
As a plush symbol
For these strange days,
When breathing the air
Without a masque on
Around others
Is unhealthy.

Little Teddy
Reassures us
That these days
Don't have to be scary.
He tells us
Non-verbally
That if we stay safe,
If we keep our connections
Despite the isolation,
Despite the miles,

EVERYTHING WILL BE OK.

Dee Allen.

On Power

When the power of love
overcomes the love of power
the world will know peace.

Attributed to Jimi Hendrix

Total U.S. deaths from COVID-19: 159,415

58

Women 6 Feet Apart

She enters through the backyard gate
carrying a basket covered with a cloth
entering the garden I greet her
wearing my pandemic mask
sitting under a shade on the patio couch
We settle into a familiar intimacy
for a comforting chat
She takes out a piece she is crocheting
as we talk
She calls it "Seedlings"
She tells me it is about her
and her recently deceased sister
We speak of grief and healing
her fingers move as a base line
to the melody of our voices
speaking from our inner themes
and deep knowledge
of each other's histories
I feel myself being snuggly stitched
into the work
by the hand-spun woolen threads
The colors merging with
our exchanged words
filling in the forced distance
strengthening our bond with love

Nina Serrano

Sea Spirits in Pandemic Times

Every day Andres sends me news on email
of the sea lions and seals
who bask on a floating pier
near the beach he visits in Alameda
He contemplates the water
seeking spiritual thoughts
that come in the rippling circles
caused by pebbles he throws

He reports "Seals and sea lions good"
and my heart rejoices to read it

Nina Serrano

August

Coffee with powdered sugar
Lukewarm tea with tangerine rind
Almond milk on toast

Mannequins on their knees
    heads bowed,
    arms locked & gripped
    in determination

Opinions nailed to the cross
Nuns crossing night rivers
    with lanterns
    and vanishing faith

(the quiet is deafening)

Fireflies light the underground
Eyes focus on evolution
Pounding hearts reflect revolution

(the quiet is deafening)

Jeannette DesBoine

Total U.S. deaths from COVID-19: 161,885

59

We

We is a strong word...
Stronger than I
Tougher than you
Bigger than one
Better than two
We is binding

We is a solution
An answer
A place
A nation
A stance
A movement
A revolution
We is freedom

We is a pact...
A healer
A merger
A tie
A connector
A refuge
A haven
We is a suit of armor
We is like cement

We is magnetic
We is a vine
It attracts and combines
It grows and supports
It weaves and links
It's a positive force
It's plan and achievement
It's roots and goals
We never stands alone

We can change the world

Jeannette DesBoine

Humanity's Fate

Fear, Covid, droplets, death
Can we crack the viral code
To save our one human race?

Black, white, racist, rage
Can we scale the hate-filled abyss
To heal our one human race?

Earth, rocks, birches, grass
Can we build a rustic nest
To nurture our one human race?

Climate, carbon, ozone, biomes
Can we discover the key
To ensure Earth's precious survival?

Or does Daffy Duck
Get the last soundbite, as he laughs,
"Whoo Hoo! Hoo Hoo!"
"That's all Folks!"

Nancy Tolin

On Solidarity

Solidarity extends far beyond sporadic acts of generosity. Instead it requires thinking in communal terms, and includes fighting structural causes of poverty. It also requires facing the destructive effects of the "empire of money."

Pope Francis, 2014

Total U.S. deaths from COVID-19: 163,528

Walk About

I walk about
in a strange new land
the ground is tilted
beneath my unsteady gait
frightened by the invisible
it could be anywhere, on anything

I walk about
in a sea of bound faces
gloved hands
sheltered hearts
no one making eye contact
common courtesies suspended

I could be anywhere
not able to recognize the familiar
apprehensive of what I don't know
denying myself tactile experience
drowning in despair

Mouth closed tight around zinc lozenges
...just in case...
an airborne infected droplet makes it way
through layers of woven fabric
and sticks to moist mucous membranes

I walk about
questioning my body's innate ability
to defend and to heal
forgetting the internal mechanisms
of the nostril to kill unwanted foe

I spend time alone
in my home
looking out at a window
hiding behind bleach wipes and hand
sanitizers
dreading a knock on the door
a friend could be a trojan horse
or a stranger for that matter

I no longer know who to trust
not the status quo
no champion to rescue me
so I stockpile essentials
hoping I can hold out
until sanity is restored

Myra Nissen

Coins and Treasures

To spend it,
       Yet not too carelessly;
To hoard it,
       Yet not too frugally;
To give it,
       Yet not too liberally;
To value it,
       Yet not too highly;
TIME—THE UNIVERSAL COIN.

To live it,
       But not too pompously;
To love it,
       But not too sensually;
To embrace it,
       But not too closely;
To leave it,
       But not too quickly;
LIFE—THE UNIVERSAL TREASURE.

Bud Light

Total U.S. deaths from COVID-19: 166,644

61

Friday, August 14, 2020
Lack

Born with No Silver Spoon

He's born in the world with none,
He's living in this world with none,
He's dying in this world with none,
He's born with no silver spoon.

    The poor man's quench is in a cheap bottle of wine,
        The poor man's a cinch for being this kind,
      The poor man's lynched of speaking his mind.

He tries for some,
He cries for some,
He dies for some,
He's born with no silver spoon.

       The poor man's dream is his reality,
     The poor man's scheme is his poverty,
    The poor man's esteem is lost in society.

His face is in misery,
His race is a mystery,
He's erased from His-Story,
He's born with no silver spoon.

     The poor man's hunger is a free meal,
     The poor man's plunder is his steal,
     The poor man's wonder is how he feels.

He's pushed astray,
He's the one for which we pray,
He's the one that loses his way,
He's the one that we forsake.

He's the one that's born and dies too soon,
He is the one that is born
With no silver spoon.

Mary "Lady-D" Brown

No Love

Sitting on the couch
Watching TV
Reaching for her thigh
But it wasn't there
The loneliness sets in
Darkness all around
No touch
No feel
No warmth
No hope
When human interaction ceases to
exist
We forget what it's like to love
To feel happiness
A little tenderness
Love is absent from America
The world
Make America love again

Galen Kusic

Total U.S. deaths from COVID-19: 169,049

Daily Battle

Day by day
We flog the wolves away
The dire wolves
That stalk our souls.

Sun-flecked water,
Crisp cleansing breezes,
Fresh lemon cheesecake left at my door,
Kindness, affection,
Lavished by strangers and neighbors,
Keep terror at bay.

Words of endearment, long stifled
Overflow the dams
Of time and distance
Long-time companions and close-held family,
Stay near with innate assurance
That our vital bonds will never fray.

Yet, each day
We see democracy
Erode and slink away
Demeaned
In the mean embrace of despotism,
Beloved community brutalized
By the scythe of division, the flashbang of fear,
People dying dying dying dreadfully
From malignant neglect and rabid virus,
Hope faltering
In the clammy wait for
Test results.

Day by day,
We cast the wolves away,
The dire wolves
That stalk our souls,
But will never drain the reservoir
Of our compassion,

Nor quell our conjoint feisty
Spirit.

Mary Susan Gast

Light, Hope, and Love

Praise the light that comes early
after the stars go out—
before the first bird wakes
and sings its joy to the setting moon.

Praise the glimmer of hope
we dream before dawn,
when night casts its shadow
along buildings and empty streets—
in dark rooms
where loneliness embraces
those who cannot sleep.

Praise love.
It is the song that stays late,
the candle that burns
after the light is gone.

Johanna Ely

Total U.S. deaths from COVID-19: 170,662

63

Calm, Schmalm

Like a belligerent drunk in a bar,
unwanted thoughts barge around my mind
looking for a fight. *Stupid Calm app.*

I'm a New Yorker trying to meditate and
my Type-A personality screams for attention:
When will this 10-minute torture end?

Perhaps a Haiku,
clever words stitched together?
I have no patience.

I have only myself to blame
for stress. Finally comes today's message:
Obstacles do not block the path.

*They **are** the path.*

Becky Bishop White

Tweet on August 15, 2020

Today in Oakland it was 91 thousand
damn degrees and now it's raining.

Go home, sky,
you're drunk.

Diana Claire Helmuth

The Swim

Red white flags lazily flutter in the breeze
   while wisps of clouds saunter by.
Trees whisper a soft tune, magic to my
   world-weary ears as I push forward.
My world at peace for a moment.
Now backwards.
Whirling water is crystalline,
   my ears submerged
   unable to discern any outer racket.
Inner turmoil continues to race
   in my veins,
Pushing thoughts to the cortex.
Cannot control the onslaught
   going forward,
Wishing for the peaceful past.

Jan Radesky

Total U.S. deaths from COVID-19: 173,731

Letter to My Great-Grandchildren

Dear Chance & Aurora,

Maybe your grandparents
told you about this, maybe not.
When they were young couples
raising your mom and dad
the world changed overnight.

One day we hiked the yellow hills
danced to jam bands
marched by the thousands in protest.
We lounged in cafes & hugged our friends
just the way you do.

But the world changed overnight.
It was like a war
everyone fighting the enemy of illness.
We had to stay at home &
walk six feet apart.

The stores were shuttered
& the theaters boarded up.
Restaurants closed
because they couldn't pay the rent.
The enemy was a virus that knew how to kill.

At first we cried, shocked with grief & fear.
Then the clocks melted.
We bit our nails & held our children close.
Some folks died, others comforted us
with their words.

Gradually, we came to our senses
& did what we could.
We found new ways to visit
read poems to our neighbors
over fences, played music in driveways.

Though parks were closed,
we still went on walks.
Everywhere, there were masked faces.
The dogs thought it funny
that humans were muzzled.

The trees sighed deep sighs
& the wildflowers
bloomed in hues we'd never seen.

Sandra Anfang

Poem for Louise

I can feel Louise riding
on her new birthday bike
pedaling right back to her girlhood
Cheeks blooming with the glow
of pumping in fresh oxygen
Steering herself in new directions
She moves swiftly
golden hair under a safe helmet
Thoughts rolling along mask and all
The exuberance of a revived skill
and a new activity
This energy reaches my mind
because I think of her
and feel refreshed

Nina Serrano

> *Total U.S. deaths from COVID-19: 175,913*

Out Front

I am grateful for...
The arched roof above my head
The twin rafters with
The twin lights, holding it in place
The four walls surrounding me
The two windows with
The two Venetian blinds, down & shut at all times
The red brick floor below my feet
The wooden shelves full of books & movies
The VHS by themselves & DVDs in clear totes
The Keetsa© mattress I sleep on
The melatonin that helps me sleep
The vegan food in my fridge, a meat-free zone
The fruit & vegetable juices I savour
The filtered water I drink more than tap
The hardcover journal notebooks and
The rollerpoint pens I use to express myself
The shower I use, even though I'm a bathtub man
The Hewlett Packard laptop computer
aiding creation of
The once and future poetry volumes
The Samsung© TV & VCR/DVD player combo
The little house in East Oakland I call home
The vast collection of political slogan t-shirts
I wear the convictions of my heart
On my chest
SOMETIMES ANTI-SOCIAL
ALWAYS ANTI-RACIST
Remains a personal favourite but
BEING BLACK IS NOT A CRIME
Gets me the most love on the street
But most of all *I am grateful for...*

The bus drivers
The firefighters
The restaurant
Delivery drivers
The subway train conductors
The launderette clerks

The grocery store workers
The farmer's market workers
Which I happen to be one
The doctors
The nurses
The paramedics
The pharmacy workers
The protestors for the rights of all Black lives
The dead and the living
The mutual aid collectives
Giving food, water, medicine and household
Items to the people living hand to
mouth
During this rotten pandemic
And long before
All the heroes
Out front
In our service
Seeing to our immediate
Survival needs
They could use the praise
And you don't need
Super powers

To be a hero
Just be there
Out front
For us—

Dee Allen.

Total U.S. deaths from COVID-19: 177,397

66

The Ghosts of You

The ghosts of your existence
Anonymous, spectral, never known,
Arrive hot and deadly in a silent fog
And surround me,
Invade my world,
Entrap me here in my air-conditioned home.

Poor me.
Not.

The particulate remnants
Of your home,
The smoldering bits
Of your walls,
The white bits of you
That gather on my car
And enter my aging lungs
Surround me whole.
These ghostly hints of your loss
Come filter my thoughts
And possess me
And haunt
What's left of everyday pursuits.

Poor me.
Not.

Yet we live with your ghosts.
Your loss is ours in miniature,
But lethal nonetheless,
A floating threat to body and soul,
Invasive in and out,
Sadly, your massive loss is now
A mind-numbing, choking, ghostly surround.

Roger Straw

Sneaker Wave

"I'm fine, thank you"

Like a sneaker wave
it can crash over you
when you look away
from the turbulent ocean of hurt
to a more peaceful horizon,
the number of things
weighing down your mind,
in an instant of unawareness
smash into your soul.

Katrina Monroe

The Power of Poetry

Shattering, evocative speech
that breaks fixed conclusions and presses
us always toward new, dangerous,
imaginative possibilities.

Rev. Dr. Walter Brueggemann
from Finally Comes the Poet

Total U.S. deaths from COVID-19: 180,288

I Remember How It Was

I remember how it was

anticipating the subtle slide into summer
my time, my favorite time, favorite season
rippled with festivals and celebrations
with blue skies and sunshine and ripening fruit
and outdoor farmer's markets
the outdoors calling, always calling to me,
"Come on, come on.
Can you come out to play?"
My heart beating fast, saying,
"Yes, yes, oh yes!"

I remember how it was
anticipating the magic of memorable dates
anniversary of our first date, May 18,
spring ski trip so many years ago
our wedding anniversary June 14,
wedding in the redwoods
his birthday, my birthday, our son's birthday
our hearts barely able to contain the joy
of June and July.

I remember how it was
anticipating the string of summer festivals
Mother's Day on Park St.,
dancing in the streets
4th of July parade and Beatle bliss with the Sun
Kings
our annual trek to the Oregon Country Fair
home to all whose hearts are open
Scottish Games, attuned to the Celtic drum beat
Hardly Strictly Bluegrass,
where an infinite sea of faces
graces Golden Gate Park.

I remember how it was
when we could all freely hug, could all be close,
could embrace each other

in the ecstatic joy of sharing together
the day, the sky, the meadows, the music,
the joy of human hearts
that drink together from the overflowing fountain
of the human spirit.

Cathy Dana

The Clumsy Giant

Pulling plants from garden soil
shaking earth from shocked roots
life in damp substrate scatters.
Even weeds are homes.
When she moves a plastic bag
full of leaves the tarantula's legs
freeze, braced against the wood
board of the raised bed, exposed,
vulnerable. Rearing up on back
legs, waving—
arched, ready to battle.

Fear: a primal focus between
both creatures.

The clumsy giant and a tarantula.

Gently pushing the bag back into
place to hide her again, she looked
into black eyes and said, "We've been
your pandemic for a long time,
haven't we?"

Georgette Howington

Total U.S. deaths from COVID-19: 182,352

68

Stand in the Chaos

How can a pandemic with worldwide casualties
be deemed a hoax?
There are those who maintain an allegiance to:
Pseudoscience, a news source, their reality,
an expert or celebrity, our American president
We are left to determine the truth.
What do we believe? How? By our experience?
By the leaders that swallow us whole?
By those who leave us wallowing in our fears
of the future?

If we do not know someone that has the
virus, is it untrue?
If we know someone that has it,
do we not question?
We rely on what we choose to listen
Or perhaps consider conspiracy theories
that sound surreal?
Surreal is the moment in which we live
What difference does it make in what we
believe?
They shatter daily
News confirms chaos
We hate to watch but need to hear,
see the devastation
Our country is drowning in debt, tears, lies,
fears, revolt, tyranny
The world in crisis

Shut out the chaos, a friend admonishes
I gather my guts, thoughts, fears
I roll them into the paperbag of my soul
My yoga teaches me: to let go
Lie down quietly, thoughtfully, clearly
Stand in your truth

Empty your mind
Stand in your power
Feel the strength of the weight in your feet,
your stance

Feel your energy of who you are

Breathe
Hear the rush of the ocean in your throat
Close your eyes and hear the wind
of the universe
It waits for you to stop, listen

Diana Tenes

My Country Calls

I hear it in the pleading eyes of children,
caged
I hear it in George Floyd's last breath
I hear it in Lady Liberty's tears

Ringing, breathless, in my ears

Vote...
⠀⠀Vote...
⠀⠀⠀⠀Vote...

Mary Harrell

> *Total U.S. deaths from COVID-19: 183,720:*

It's One of Those Days

Thirty minutes before a lunch-time Zoom
cat gets out
Who left the door ajar?
It's one of those days

Four walls surround a small patio
one way in—same way out
Door latches from behind
It's one of those days

We're both locked out
barefoot, keyless, phone inside
Neighbor responds to my cries
Maybe things will be OK

Her phone's expired
She passes a ladder across the fence
one way up, no way down
It's one of those days

Another passes a phone
manager can come at four
Can I come before noon?
It's one of those days

Another has a ladder to offer
I climb up one and down the other
Over the fence now
It may be a better day

Offered a spare mask
she takes me to the rental office
Feet bare and face covered
A key in hand and on my way

A quarter hour to spare
bring in the cat

get on the call
As if nothing happened at all

Myra Nissen

A Certain Silence

the alternative is not dishonest,
but rather a certain silence,
which is very different from
a certain quiet,
all eyes watching,
even if smaller than stones,
held in place by swirling winds,
for if only,
circle be;
oval become,
no inter-stices, slices,
brought home,
none but granted
nights folly upon tiny gnome,
standing,
laying,
moving
or
not;
if at all leaving this
wrapped gravity
behind
the history of it all.
rubrics gnomon, humm
hyme.
stand together
swaying
alone.

Tom Stanton

Total U.S. deaths from COVID-19: 186,397

Dry Lightning

Oh California, where are you burning?

From the cabin porch,
I search the horizon through haze and trees.
The deck rails I stained only yesterday,
with their cut-out pattern of swallows in flight,
glow orange in this strange amber light.

How will we know if we need to go?
What can we save?
What will be lost?
How many others are caught
in the urgency of these choices?

Where do the flames hunger and seethe?
Where do the deer run for their lives
as the great firs ignite and fall?
How many fires must the land withstand
before we find our way?

Oh California, where are you burning?

Deborah Bachels Schmidt

Perfect Pitch

i too sing america...
and i have sung this song long & hard...my
tone deliberate...the tune forced...the melody
chipped, cracked & worn...chords twisted,
crushed, & ground to squeak, squeal, &
scream.
i sing.

i too sing america...
i sing in the key of death...

death by lynching...death by design...death by
policy...death by policing...death by
decree...death...
i sing...

i too sing america...but i didn't write the
song...nor is it well written. its lyrics are lies
but i sing this foreign song & i sing LOUD. i
want the world to hear. i want the globe to
see. i want the planet to watch my lips
move...to follow my eyes as i survey the choir
& study the choir director.

of thee i sing...
the piano is poorly tuned...the soloist tone
deaf...but still he sings...and i too sing
america...but I sing in perfect pitch.

Jeannette DesBoine

War Hero, Then and Now

Shades drawn against the heat
windows closed against the smoke
hiding from the unseen virus
in his apartment
as he did years ago in a war bunker
he feels
invisible.
Remembering the days when he
survived against a known enemy
and greater odds
and felt
invincible.

Katrina Monroe

Total U.S. deaths from COVID-19: 188,377

71

Sunday, September 6, 2020
Longing

Where Does Hope Live?

I haven't been there in seven weeks.
My school. My classroom.
The room with empty chairs now
because of the pandemic.
The room hung with a mobile of birds,
a rainbow of birds,
made by one of my shyest students.
The room with the brightly colored prayer flags
made by my class,
strung across the room, flashing turquoise,
purple, orange, yellow, green
splashed with sequins and jewels
and butterflies and feathers
and messages of hope.
The room with thank you notes to me,
some scribbled,
some painstakingly drawn by my students.
The room with a desk full of scissors, pens,
glue sticks, tape,
student work so beautiful I just couldn't
throw it out,
and a clear plastic jar full of fruit-flavored
hard candies in shiny wrappers,
waiting for me to give them out
when my students have worked hard.
The room where my "Poetry Rocks" sign
and seven anthologies
of student poetry are lined up,
proclaiming the glory of poetry.
I haven't been there in seven weeks
to see their faces, hear the funny things they say,
catch them in an "aha!" moment.
I see them now on Zoom meetings, some of them,
and we talk and share and I know they're still
out there.
I haven't been there in seven weeks
and I miss them.

Hope lives in me when I think of them.
May their prayer flags shine like beacons of hope
to the world.

Cathy Dana

Icarus in the 21ST Century

At the water's edge, swaths of red, yellow, orange
  and green cover the wild grasses
Rising on the wind, rumpled sails puff
  into crescents
Anime rainbows suspended overhead
Tethered pilots dance like marionettes
Feet skimming the ground
Tugging at the billowing sail as it tacks
  from side to side

Yellow sail lifts first, hovers, flaps,
  sags and plummets,
Crumpling on the ground like a discarded pupa
Orange sail launches and climbs
Riding the current out to the Strait
Shimmering blue water below reflecting an array
  of silver pixels

The eye of the osprey
Holds the flying machine in its sights
As it dives, circles and soars
Between sea and sun
Free at last

Kathleen Herrmann

Total U.S. deaths from COVID-19: 189,604

Hello. My Name is Courage!

How do you smile after so many deaths?
When innocent loved ones are murdered
in their homes?
In their beds seeking rest from the day before.

How do you smile after so many deaths?
Murdered by them boys in blue.
Kneed down on necks.
Bodies beaten black and blue over $20.

How many times do the innocent have to
scream, "I Can't Breathe?"
When will the innocent be heard?

And in times like these, poetic verse bandages
peel off too easy!
It can't change actions passed down
400 years later.

Ancestors speak!
My mama instinct has been triggered.
So naturally, I provide shelter.
My babies have learned to duck & cover.
Under Eagles' wings.

It takes courage to smile.
After all the deaths, I have forgotten how.
It sometimes hurts to try.

No amount of therapy sessions can help me
remember why I should.

Because I REFUSE to smile until justice is
served!!!

Aqueila M. Lewis-Ross

We All

We all saw
a man herded, felled,
and held to the ground like a wild animal.
We all heard
his last pleas for breath
as his life force was extinguished.
We all felt
the anger searing our bodies like a hot knife,
that hot knife now burning holes
in the thin veil of fabric over our land.

Some take a knee
in sorrow and remorse
recognizing the need for unity and change.
Some self-righteously fan the flames
as if this fire could be put out
by setting multiple cross fires.
Some of us cower inside
already fragile in a pandemic
broken in spirit
mourning that our tears cannot douse
the nation's flames
nor our silence sew back a society's soul.

Katrina Monroe

Total U.S. deaths from COVID-19: 191,507

Friday, September 11, 2020
Air supply

Nectar

Late August morning,
My once-vibrant garden cries out in distress,
Cries out for water, love and attention.
Sun-starved and smoke-drenched from wildfires,
Everything's wilting in the toxic, unbreathable air.
I emerge from the sliding glass door,
Wearing a large N95 mask, dark sunglasses,
And my wide-brimmed, purple sun hat—
Looking like a giant, Kafkaesque insect.
A brave hummingbird zips toward the birdfeeder,
But then stops and hovers near me,
Studying me, deciding if it is safe
To sip nectar with me so close by.

I smile behind my mask, amused that the lovely,
Iridescent winged-bird does not recognize me.
I want to say, "Hey, I'm not a cockroach—
I'm that two-legged creature who nurtures
The garden and refills the nectar
In your birdfeeder."
But even my purple hat looks dusky today
With all that smoke.

And the bird darts to the plum tree
And lights on a high branch,
To wait for this giant cockroach
To leave.

Nancy Tolin

Morning Light September 9

We woke inside an amber honeycomb
Suffused with the amaranth pink of dawn,
As harsh wildfire smoke
Hovered above
A stubborn marine layer
That rebuffed the tiniest flecks of sooty vapor
While hardier chunks of ash fell unchecked
From the smudged vermilion sky.

Mary Susan Gast

On Life

Remember that there is meaning
beyond absurdity. Know that every deed
counts, that every word is power...
Above all, remember that you must build
your life as if it were a work of art.

Rabbi Abraham Joshua Heschel

Total U.S. deaths from COVID-19: 193,587

Compassion Survives

A destitute man crouched under the causeway connecting the drugstore and Safeway. He'd squeezed his emaciated frame between the watermelon and cantaloupe bins. The causeway provided a shield from the blistering sun, but no relief from the 90° heat. He wore ragged jeans, dilapidated shoes, and a faded T-shirt, rife with holes.

"Hi there," I began, "Can I get you something to eat?"

"O K-K-K," he stuttered.

Once inside, I purchased a sandwich, a soda and a bottle of hand sanitizer.

But, when I returned, he'd left, so I deposited the items where he'd been sitting.

I went to Safeway more often than usual over the next week. When he was there, it was the same as before. So, I'd just wave, and head into the store.

One day, he nodded at me as I went by and didn't glance furtively behind me as he did so.

"At last!" I thought, and repeated what had now become a mantra, "If you've left already, I'll just leave some things right here."

A few days after that, he waved at me as I was returning to my car. I caught just the hint of a smile from him. He'll never know that, with that simple grin, he'd given me more than I ever could have given him.

Carol Gieg

Mind with the Wind

Dancing leaves
Rolling waves
Mind with the wind
Take us far away
To a distant land
One where we can ALL say
That we get along
Painted trees
Lovely reeds
Together, we are paired
Simple, complex and rare
And when we come back from that land,
  my friend
We'll ALL be better in the end

Galen Kusic

Last Message

Walk with the wind, brothers and sisters, and let the spirit of peace and the power of everlasting love be your guide.

John Lewis, from "Together, You Can Redeem the Soul of our Nation"

Total U.S. deaths from COVID-19: 194,738

Each New Day

Each new day
is new space
a chance to choose.

A change of pace?
Enlightenment? Sharing grace?
Or
Hiding away? Isolation?
you lose.

Free time is ethereal.
to be received
as a gift
a chance to dance
Or
cold cereal
immaterial.

Are we in a race?
To what?
salvation? stagnation? altercation?
Or
Exploration.

Maybe you have something to say
Say it.
Maybe you want to dance
Take a chance
Turn up the music
and dance.

Each new day
Is new space
a chance to choose.

A train rushing past
Stopping only for passengers
A fleeting chance
We can get on board
Dance.

It's a wonderful life
new challenges
a chance to rise
we can adapt
be better or bitter.

Each new day
Is new space.

Beth Grimm

And Now It's Morning

I wake, open the door to the outside,
hoping to smell fresh morning breezes.
Instead, the smoky air
from hundreds of fires
burns my nostrils.

I shut the door quickly.
How strange to gaze at my backyard
through glass,
to watch the end of summer pass
in this smoke-filled haze.
No hummingbirds at the feeder.

Johanna Ely

Total U.S. deaths from COVID-19: 197,331

Coronavirus Pandemic

(*written in early April when Italian hospital staff
had to choose who they would allow to die*)

Dear Sick Italian Octogenarians
I too am over 80
It saddens me that you
will be allowed to die
from lack of hospital facilities
I hope the effects of the illness
are not so horrendous
that you still can have
peace to review your life
be satisfied and ready
to leave the hospital bed
medicine and care
for the next younger person's turn
at this precious thing called life
It is all you have ever known since birth
I hope feelings of gratitude and graciousness
overwhelm you in your last breaths
and your soul leaves your body
feeling love

Nina Serrano

COVID 19

(*written March 11, 2020*)

How many will die by virus?
How many will die by gun?
How many will starve to death?

Under siege.

Jeannette DesBoine

Signs of Love

It's in their thick stolid branches,
their aged elephantine bark,
the myriad creatures who find shelter
in their ample canopies.

It's in the steady unquestioning way
they exhale oxygen for our animal lungs
and whisper their warnings
through networks of roots.

Not that fierce adoration
we humans reserve for our kindred—
more like the gardener's graceful devotion
year after year, cultivating a harvest.

This morning, as I plod by underneath them
breathing smoke-tainted air through a disposable mask
I gaze up at their branches, outstretched above me
and pause to revel in their impartial embrace.

Tamar Enoch

Total U.S. deaths from COVID-19: 199,112

Sunday, September 20, 2020
Tolls and gifts

Living With / Living Without

If a year ago you would have asked me
what I can live without
There is no doubt
That I would have confidently, boldly,
almost in a shout declared
I don't know
I mean
certainly between the inevitable
ebb and flow of life
and the close but not quite
living the dream of career, house, kids and wife
I have accepted that
I have to spend 8-9 hours a day
with people who if I was fired or retired
would likely not find me to see or say "hey"
in exchange for the 3-4 hours
with the two little people I would cease my life
or yours for
before the ink dries on this pad
the letters in DAD
often feel like an acronym for
Dogged and Distant
to feed, clothe and shelter them
takes a level of persistence
paired with a palpable and precise insistence
on denying the impact that my absence
has inflicted
pre-pandemic
you couldn't have told me that I wasn't
super present
But since having to shelter in place
I have noticed that my place of shelter
is more helter skelter than I would like to admit
And if I take a step back a bit
Covid-19 has exposed that
at least a few years prior to 2019
aspects of my life were gasping for air
it look the longest year of my life
to demonstrate to just how much
I was longing for one
different than the one I constructed

how can I return to the office suite
denying myself the sweet faces of my children
riding scooters or running in the park midday
not losing hours of my life
commuting on the freeway
I can live without the rat race
without the digitization
of my mother and grandfather's face
without the absence of a warm embrace
or if I am completely honest a cold one
a loud annoying fight
with the in-person chance to make it alright
I can live without
living without
all the things that pre-pandemic
I was living without
That mental, physical and emotional drought
so I suppose
the real question is
what can I
and what am I
willing to live with

Brandon L. Greene

Pandemic 2020

Overnight, a world of isolates.

More suicides in three months
than in an average year.

Deborah L. Fruchey

Total U.S. deaths from COVID-19: 200,105

Asylum

They are people like you; me; like all of us.
They are mothers, fathers, sons, daughters,
aunts, uncles, ancestors & descendants. They
live and let live. They bleed and die. They sing
songs, write poetry, and pray. They cook, clean,
and sew. They build houses and change tires.
They are doctors, lawyers, students, teachers,
entrepreneurs, and uncommon laborers. They
are products of the Creator. They laugh and
cry just like you and I. They...are us!

Jeannette DesBoine

Judgement Call

Slipping through the reeds of widely-woven life,
Ruth Bader Ginsburg entered the Beyond
As Rosh Hashanah began.
Evidence, as if we weren't already convinced,
That she was a rare and splendid tzaddik,
A person,
(oh, yes, "person,"
in the full-blown
14th Amendment
grand egalitarian
meaning of the word)
A person of great righteousness.

Sound the shofar,
The alarm, the wake-up call
Of ancient and uncertain tone
That hails the new year.

Hear the shofar, the blaring animal horn
That gives voice to fears and prayers
So deep inside us
There are no words.

Blow the shofar
One hundred times a day
Until we heed its rousting call
To justice and compassion.

Ruth Bader Ginsburg,
Your accomplishments
   transformed our body politic,
Your dissents
   illuminate our consciousness,
Your memory will be a blessing,
And may it also be a shofar,
Calling us, never silenced,
To battle the forces of
   oppression and exploitation
Until well-being flourishes,
For earth and all its peoples.

Shana Tovah. A good new year.
May it be a year of good.

Mary Susan Gast

Total U.S. deaths from COVID-19: 202,638

79

In the Land of Zeros and Ones

Sound waves echo back and forth through
the electrical grids. Microphones on mute;
astute teachers stare at the kids. Listen to
me; sit down; not a sound; this is your
online class; do your work to pass.

2020 has flipped its lid. We Zoom in and
out of the grid to mute our microphone,
only to log out and feel all alone, walking
out with the task to wear a mask, only to
repeat into the bleak.

Roll call; 2020, Jordan, Lennie, and Bennie.
This is where up is down and everything
upside down, turn around, inside out and
all about. The work is tons, in the world of
zeros and ones.

James Quinn

Spellbound

In that darkest hour before daybreak
We watched from the upstairs window
Jagged lightning bolts lacerating violet sky
Illuminating frozen tableaux
of Carquinez Bridge and Crockett hills
in flickering strobe flashes

Petulant Zeus was taking aim
Plucking iridescent arrows from his quiver
And hurling them to earth
with a muscular heave
Craggy slashes searing the August night

We gaped, blowing soft "oh's"
As the thunder rolled away, we slumbered

Raindrops tapping at the edges of our dreams
Beyond the hovering black-chinned hummingbird
A stagnant gray miasma hangs
Charred DNA of yesterday's normal
Doors and windows sealed against
its leaden stench

Airborne strikes
Boots on the ground
Puny weapons against the insatiable dragon
Red sun rising
Sorrowful eyes seek the phoenix

From our safe perch
We watched the ghastly spectacle detonate
Spellbound

Kathleen Herrmann

Fire

Evacuation packing:
what to never see again?

Deborah L. Fruchey

Total U.S. deaths from COVID-19: 204,479

Time and seasons

Autumn 2020

I used to call it "fall"
now known to me as "fire season"
as ghostly ash snows on parked cars
and the last
of the growing tomatoes and squashes
I often joined in conversations about
if it was wise
to give trick-or-treaters candy
You can forget door-to-door visitors
with shelter in place
Material conditions preempt tradition
All my age-old seasonal expectations
dissolved in confusion
after the day
that Day did not follow night
When it stayed night most of the day
with an orange sky
Change which was always
what I could count on
is now what I can count on
I am relearning what it means
to live in the present
A tough lesson
minute by minute

Nina Serrano

The Road Ahead

There are many miles we travel
Wondering if the road's a shadow;
Searching for some new tomorrow
While willing to concede
That this road we're on
Has its unique and real sorrow:
So please tell us if perhaps
There is a brighter and healthier tomorrow
Or is yesterday during this virus
Just a day I borrowed.

Bud Light

Time, 2020

The days lumber by,
Blind giants,
With bungling fingers too thick
  to pick daisies,
Elephantine feet too plodding
  to dance.

Mary Susan Gast

Total U.S. deaths from COVID-19: 205,579

A Sunflower
Is Just as Pretty
as a Rose

Black Sunflowers stand tall.
Today, they Rise.
Standing taller than ever.

Adorned by the ancestors' plight.
Blood spilt centuries ago,
Has spilt over still.
Footprints leave a trail of tears
Imprints reappear.

Black Sunflowers continue to grow
as blood spills over.
So many are dying.
Hung like Xmas tree ornaments.
Kinda forgot Summer was here.
Spring was barely celebrated
Fear of the unknown
A people, well-groomed were stuck
Displaced.
Mandated to shelter-in-place.

How can one be happy with all this mess?
As much as we long to unmask,
Black Sunflowers are still oppressed!

See the Banto Knots!
Red, Black, & Green Frocks!
Children frolic in water parks!
Until the Sun lays down to rest.
Unfolding of its petals
A glorious work of art
Shows a glimpse of past lives lived.
Mirroring the sun.

Oh how I adore thee!
Black Sunflowers are the Light!

And like Sunflowers symbolize adoration,
loyalty and longevity;
A Rose Will Always Be A Rose!

But a when a Black Sunflower transforms,
People better be ready!

The Marches must continue on!
Let the Youth Speak!
Summer is finally here!

And the Black Sunflower is not going anywhere!
I never really paid attention to Sunflowers before.
Now after all this,
they're my favorite type of flower!

Aqueila M. Lewis-Ross

Pandemic Mismanagement

Americans expected to stretch $1200.
Unemployment breaks the scale.
Evictions mount. A nation on the run.
Passport denied.
Nowhere to hide from this virus.
Millions infected. Over 200,000 dead.
The safety net sent to the shredder
as Congress dawdles—
their perfectionism prevents payments.
The president golfs and gaslights.
His supporters flaunt the law.
No end in sight to this motorcade of death.
Wake me when it's safe to hug again.

D.L. Lang

> Total U.S. deaths from COVID-19: 207,741

Friday, October 2, 2020
How long

Them

Everybody's in charge and nobody's in charge
and nothing is getting done...
And the whole world is spinning out of
control and chaos is second to none.

States of confusion pave our roads
while we dance at the edge of extinction...
And we sing a song that makes no sense
to the courage of our convictions.

We take to our knees to some bellowing
noise while the whisper of God is lost...
And the louder the noise the darker the
storm and we weep as we burn in regret.

Long lines of losers grab gusto
and scurry up the bandwagon...
And we punch their ticket and stand aside
as we vanish in the thick of it.

Everybody's in charge and nobody's in charge
and we leave things up to THEM...
A THEM we don't know. A THEM we can't
trust. A THEM riding herd
on the rest...

The rest being us...the ones being crushed
under the heel of hate...
And we close our eyes and button our lips
and we wait, and we wait, and we wait...

Mistake!

Jeannette DesBoine

A Cry from Psalm 94

How long, O Author of Life,
How long shall the exploiters,
How long shall the self-serving exult,
And pour out their contemptuous words,
Callously boasting of the abuse they inflict?
They crush Your people, O Holy One,
 and afflict Your very own.
They kill the defenseless and the stranger,
They murder the orphan...

Can corrupt governments be allied with You,
Framing misery by statute,
Banding together against the fullness of life,
Condemning the faithful to death?

Rise up, O Renewal of the earth;
Let the arrogant receive their due!

*Mary Susan Gast, from "Redemption Songs, A
21st Century Descant on the Psalms"*

Total U.S. deaths from COVID-19: 209,465

Sunday, October 4, 2020
Expression from the core

Give an Artist a Canvas

Give an artist a canvas.
And freedom to create as they please.
Practice makes perfect.

My body was the canvas.
At first to be used to harm.
Cells held on to pain from generations past.
Ancestors spoke truth to power
 in and through me.
It glowed from within.
Became my protection.
Adding another layer of gray-haired wisdom!

Paint me gold
Carrying riches buried in treasures never
opened.
See the key?
Rich people always hide it in unattainable
places.

Paint me liquefied.
Fluid as water.
Blue-green like the ocean.
A favorite color.
Peaceful.
Tranquil.
I could stay here until pruning
no longer is beautiful on skin.

Saw a post about a mama who made
rainbow spaghetti for dinner!
Wish I were that creative or had the energy
 to be this dedicated.
But, I will do anything
to see my little princess smile!

Paint me rainbow.
May I shine bright for all to see!

Aqueila M. Lewis-Ross

Seasons of Grief

This is the season of grieving Black mothers
 Who grieve for what is
 Who grieve for what isn't

This is the season of grieving Black mothers
 Who grieve for change
 Who grieve the unchanged

This is the season of grieving Black mothers
 Who grieve the present, the past, and the future
 Who grieve for their daughters
  as well as their sons

This is the season of grieving Black mothers
 Who grieve for all children murdered and sullied
 Who grieve for hopes—dead and gone

This is the season of grieving Black mothers
 Who grieve a democracy—rancid and septic
 Who grieve a justice—corrupt and inept

This is the season of grieving Black mothers
 Who grieve a great nation castrating itself

Jeannette DesBoine

Total U.S. deaths from COVID-19: 210,533

Wednesday, October 7, 2020
Disturbance

*"i think so
i feel a terror
a new fear...."*

"Oft Aoctober Night"

J. Edgar.
J. Edgar.
......
J.....
Let's just call him "jay."
This is for "jay."

Tunnel,
Moving,
Sliding, slipping,
......tunneling!

Slipping, sliding, slipping tunnel.

Dark hole changing size,
light coming through it.

pin hole,
pin hole,
rotary door closing.

pin hole.
pin hole.
.... oh mr. Prufrock!

Prufrock!
Prufrock!

...........This for jay Edgar
jay Edgar

I was in a car wreck last night;
And after the silence and
the sprinkling of the glass;

I sat in the field and,

I turned the lights in my head off;
walked around ...;
....I really didn't see anything;
.......and I walked away;....

•(a friend said:)"You are still in shock."
*"i think so
i feel a terror
a new fear...."*

Tom Stanton

A Tuesday Text

I won't be bogged down in the reasons why...
For, when I looked up in today's sky...
I saw the sun...
And...it was...
one in vermillion...
again...

Genea Brice

Total U.S. deaths from COVID-19: 212,634

dark matter

these are days of dark matter...

days when it is treasonous to utter phrases
like "black lives matter" and to expect equal
treatment under the law-of-the-land...

days when democracy has
regressed...returned to her
kakistocracy...reverted to her cloak, her
hood, her burning crosses, her cowardice,
and her KKKlan...

these are days when evil is condoned...where
blatant lies are ritual...where logic is null and
void...reason is counterproductive...the
constitution is toilet paper...justice is a
cartoon...and terror brandishes a nine iron...

these are days of dark matter

Jeannette DesBoine

After the Grenade
Went Off—2016
[with a nod to Walt Whitman and Bob Marley]

Stupefied by the flashbang verdict
Of the electoral vote,
I questioned whether I had ever heard
America singing.

Sweet land of liberty, of thee we sang?
Odes to courage, anthems to equality.

Or was I mistaken?
Those varied carols I thought I'd heard—

Were they calamitously off-pitch distortions
That overran my gullible innermost ear?

Did the electors validate an America yearning
To sing
In the key of gloating,
To sing
To the beat of disdain?
With derisive and divisive words
Unlyrically belittling, Scorning harmony and
Muting counterpoint?

*Now's the time to sing
Our songs of freedom
And solidarity,
Our songs of freedom,
Redemption songs,
Our songs of freedom.*

Mary Susan Gast

Total U.S. deaths from COVID-19: 214,594

86

Rebirth and the Statue

What's under those flowing robes?
Yearning to breathe free…

What's your inner flame,
Beckoning…

Your hope shines bright for distant shores
And you dream of lives that welcome more.

Progenitor Liberty
Giving life to fleeing millions

Your womb embraces
All who enter willingly,
Flee tyranny
Build, for democracy
For a land of the brave and free.

In this dark age
This Trumpian autocracy…
Give of yourself,
Rebirth us
With your generative loving arms
To immigrate again
To our own shores.

What's under those flowing robes?
The lasting casting of promise,
The lifeblood of a borning nation,
Stilled, yet ever flowing free.

Roger Straw

Letter

Dear Future,
  Will you be there for me?

Anonymous 12-year-old

The New Colossus

Not like the brazen giant of Greek fame,
With conquering limbs astride
  from land to land;
Here at our sea-washed, sunset gates
  shall stand
A mighty woman with a torch, whose flame
Is the imprisoned lightning, and her name
Mother of Exiles. From her beacon-hand
Glows world-wide welcome;
  her mild eyes command
The air-bridged harbor that twin cities frame.
"Keep, ancient lands, your storied pomp!"
  cries she
With silent lips.
"Give me your tired, your poor,
Your huddled masses yearning to breathe free,
The wretched refuse of your teeming shore.
Send these, the homeless, tempest-tossed
  to me,
I lift my lamp beside the golden door!"

Emma Lazarus, 1883

Total U.S. deaths from COVID-19: 215,712

Leilani

Yesterday the smoky air cleared
I visited my new 7th great grandchild
for the first time
wearing a mask
Gathering safely in the lush garden
of ripe peaches figs squashes
pumpkins and tomatoes
As monarchs and hummingbirds flit
among the flowers.
Seated I held her mellow and beautiful being
in my arms
and said her name Leilani aloud
"Sweet Leilani heavenly flower" I sang to her
but could not catch her infant's smell
through the mask
Peering into her face searching for resemblances
I saw different elusive family members race by
in her random expressions
She fit so snugly against my body
as if she had always been there
Tho' only 18 days old she always had
When her mother spoke she turned towards her
Soon was nursing contentedly
in her tender embrace
falling peacefully asleep
I left with a bag of sweet ripe peaches
My heart full
The word resilient on my mind.

Nina Serrano

Homage to R.B.G.

She held back the storm alone,
and we knew she was a hero,
but we didn't know
how lonely it would feel
standing here without her.

She didn't get upset about it,
just did what she needed to do,
pretending when she had to,
because her goal was freedom.

That's all that mattered—
not being tied down
to some man's idea of a life—
winning justice, undoing the chains,

and now they can't wait
to put her memory in the ground,
now that she can no longer
face them down

with her steely eyes,
her strength that finally failed her.
She knew they were waiting,
even if we didn't.

Mary Eichbauer

Total U.S. deaths from COVID-19: 217,895

They Propped the Dead Man Up:
an Allegory

We were waist deep in the big muddy
and the big fool said to push on.
—Pete Seeger, "Waist Deep in the Big Muddy"

A man I used to know
who knew a man I used to know
told me a story about
the old man's funeral.
How they propped him up
in his single bed like a child's
dressed him in his favorite
cowboy shirt, hat, & boots.
How their feet carved circles
in the small front room
of his cabin, how they passed
around the punch, dished up
the casseroles, poured the wine.
All the while, he lay in his bed
in the corner, where it had been wheeled
watching them enjoy the feast.
He didn't miss a beat.
He looked great—alive as you or me
said the man I used to know.
Maybe a little ashen.
"They propped the dead man up"
cycles through my brain
like a country refrain.
If they hadn't heard the story
of how his Kawasaki overshot
the freeway bridge—a suspected
heart attack the cause—
you might have thought he was
enjoying an afternoon nap.
This scenario would not
be hard to replicate:
(an old man waving from
the window of an SUV;
the steel-spiked wall of his dissembling).
During the parsing of the meatloaf

the news, & the deviled eggs
they propped the dead man up
and life continued
more or less as it had before.

Sandra Anfang

No Longer

No longer
are these our fundamental rights.
No longer
is it life, liberty and the pursuit of happiness.

Now
our fundamental right
is to know the truth.
Now
life, liberty and the opportunity for happiness
follow the Truth.

Will Emes, Jr.

Total U.S. deaths from COVID-19: 219,693

89

Sunday, October 18, 2020
How can it be

2020 Wardrobe

Online shopping spree
Zoom-ready, "waist-up" clothing—
Casual, business, flirty
Pajamas below
Hair accessories, lipstick, jewelry
No pants, no face masks
Is the *virtual statement look*…complete?
Does this make me look
Casual chic or dowdy?

Wait—does this make me look FAT?
And are those JOWLS ??
Quick, put up the Zoom placard,
The one that says "under construction"

Nancy Tolin

When Will This Be Over?

When will this be over?
Aaaarrrgh….
The morning Trump show,
Ghastly and sick,
The daily covid-count
Ever-expansive,
Statewide, cross-country and world,
The frickin' fallout from
Racism, murders and mayhem…
The mob mentality that worships guns
And money
And backs the dictatorial rule of the
righteous right…

When will this be over?
A time ago, a long time,
Some of us elders lived through
Bull Connor's hoses and dogs,
Assassinations,
And a presidential eviction.

The tidal wave of horror
Wouldn't end
And then it did…
Or so we thought.

When will this be over?
The days of glory
We hoped for,
The dream days,
The visionary days,
The youthful possibility of utopia…
The faith-borne hope against hope against
hope…
Are these unreal, and lost,
Things of some unknown forever gone?

When will this be over?

Roger Straw

Total U.S. deaths from COVID-19: 220,956

90

Wednesday, October 21, 2020
In need

The Days

It's a thought.
like in the 1920s
"backwards was not an option"
Until it became an option.
Quite suddenly.
This time has been changed forever.
It is an opportunity to build a new option.
Best to take the opportunity,
rather than have to be left at the station.
Watching ourselves go by.
Probably less drinking
and less driving
would best prepare us physically
and mentally;
As we rush into this new age.
"The future is now."
Don't let it pass us by.
Please.

Tom Stanton

Respite

Fog elbowed ash away,

The sky shone blue on Friday,
Eye-cleansing cerulean,
Some free-form clouds,
No vermillion frown skulking on the horizon.

The air so clean
My lungs sang and my blood danced with oxygen.

The mighty Strait,
Our connection to the ocean,
Flowed without a care,
Sparkling gleefully.

Mary Susan Gast

Music

What we need is music—written by master mathematicians and blended by the artists of all time...Picasso, Rubens, Van Gogh, Bernard.

Harmonious music...mixed by great chefs and stirred by mama in her cozy kitchen and papa at his outdoor grill.

Melodious music...all voices on key...all directed by grandiose brilliance with an ear for tune and tone.

We need a song that everyone sings...a choir in which everybody solos...where performance is shared and each chord depends on every voice fused together like fine wine and tantalizing cheese.

The music must be served on a level platter...level and circular...circular being key...a wheel within a wheel.

And the sound must be heard globally...each voice clear and reverberating the commitment of conjoined souls...in league with one another and so focused on peace and freedom that the music becomes one single note...a tone...pitch...a bell resonating universal language.

Jeannette DesBoine

Total U.S. deaths from COVID-19: 223,532

An Abundance of Caution, April 2020

There is no *simple* any more...
no simple trip to the store or pharmacy,
no simple get-togethers with family or friends.
We are aliens in a strange new world,
where the road to the new "normal" is lined
with fear and uncertainty.

The rules are changeable and confusing,
and why is it the more they tell us to distance
the more we crave human interaction?
I wave at the mailman, the garbage collector,
and every neighbor I pass on the street,
despite my mask.
Alienation and loneliness have become
constant companions.

Even language has been altered at the gate.
We've had to grasp the meaning
of *PPE's, flattening the curve, contact tracing*
as if they are foreign vocabulary.
We have become seasoned Zoom masters.

It is painful to hear the stories of lives upended;
desperate, ordinary people struggling,
some coping with the untimely
loss of loved ones.
And there is not yet an end date
visible on the horizon.

So in *an abundance of caution*,
eat chocolate every day,
use the good silver,
take out that bottle of *Domaine Chandon*
you've been saving,
and slow dance whenever you get the chance.

Joanne Jagoda

It Doesn't Make Sense

It dawned on me several times these days
That if it's true that what they say,
Means all of us are in this together
In both fair and oft-times stormy weather;
I wonder
Then where is everybody?

This sure seems like a real war;
With an adversary like none before
And in war, it's not who's RIGHT
It's who is LEFT at the end of the fight.
A battle that, through day and night
We seem to resist and lose real sight
Of how to win this horrific fight
WHICH WE ARE LOSING.

Bud Light

Total U.S. deaths from COVID-19: 225,387

92

Rain in the Time of Plague

I

Its curtain falls gentle as a quarantine from God
that keeps souls tidied away from rain and
one another's faces.

Rain baffles down.

Its oratorio
complains of nothing,
fears nothing,
and nothing can resist.

And I?

I praise and thank grace
to keep me and you well indoors and warm
as others of us cower in holey tarps and tents
in helter-skelter shelter from the domination
of the reign of the plague and the rain.

It rains convincingly as I on dry paper write—
what thanks can match such fortune
and such favor?

Anything that falls from a thousand feet
falls to death.

Save rain that damages in striped tumble
no one and nothing.

II

Plague
scorches
Earth.

And with its reins The Old Cloaked
Coachman drives us into stalls
and stalls everything, each and everyone
for once everywhere the same.

Listen, O listen, you blessèd who read this ink
that on this page
falls clear as rain

and
black
as plague.

Take courage.
Take shelter in the shelter of our common cause
for once.

III

For in this inundation, O World, we hold
handless hands.

We join the drenched in ample consideration
for each other now.

Peace, sweet ones.
I cannot stop speaking.
I cannot bear to let you go.

Our shelter is we are the leaves of every tree
in one tree.

Thus do we bless the blessing of the plague—
its safety our sequester.

For that which curtains us choirs us.

Plague's separation joins us.

This pestilential deluge for a time
your heart with all hearts unites—
hidden—
hidden away in song,
in a chant
we all chant.
protected.

Then
rest.

Bruce Moody

Total U.S. deaths from COVID-19: 226,802

Late October Wind
Amidst This Pandemic-Pre-Election Storm

It's rattlin' m' bones,
the late-October wind
battering the roses,
shivering my skin,
twisting the hibiscus,
howling through the doors,
moaning through the windows amidst this
pandemic-pre-election storm
threatening our democracy,
dismantling sacred norms,
abandoning facts and integrity,
in eerie, foreboding tones.

Ramona Lappier

Freefall
(For President Jimmy Carter's 96th Birthday)

We have waited four hard years
To rescue our battered country
From the petulant man-child
Whose toxic whims, psychotic rants
  and routine chaos
Jettisoned our proud democracy into a
bottomless freefall
Three tiers of governance eroded to fragile
partisan facades

Oh, how we have waited
To make our mark
To make it right
Not so fast…

Mail it and risk fraud
Show up and risk health
Black and brown voters endure
  hours on their feet

Defying Jim Crow's shadow

Drop boxes are endangered in Texas and Ohio
Bogus ones appear in California
Iran, Russia and China hedge their bets

Jimmy, with your slow smile
  and unassuming manner
You have restored strangled voices
From Sierra Leone to Bangladesh
Now you stand with us
Forming a more perfect union
We, the people, will speak at last

Kathleen Herrmann

After It's Over

Give us rich soil
Where we can bury
The foulness of failure,
Where we can lay to rest
The torment of loss,
Where we can build memorials
Befitting the eternal span of
Compassion and justice,
Affection and commitment,
Where we can plant
The green seedlings
Of reconciliation to
Our history and
Our future.

Mary Susan Gast

Total U.S. deaths from COVID-19: 229,357

Friday, October 30, 2020
"Trick or . . ."

A Pandemic Halloween

Trick and treaters should beware
Covid-19's everywhere.
Ghosts and goblins all around;
Everybody's going underground!
Chaos in the word abounds
People jump at every sound.
Poltergeists in every room
Prophesize impending doom!
Skeletons in all our clothes
Our universe in sad repose

Life has reached a frantic pace
Everybody needs their space
Pollution causes trees to wilt
While nations justify their guilt

Everybody's up in arms;
Freedom fighters sound alarms
Science fiction, star wars dreams
Result in monolithic schemes

Negotiations all in shambles;
While leaders double talk, and ramble
Catastrophic, claustrophobic;
A population growing aerobic;
Our monetary niche to carve...
Who cares as millions starve!

Predictions of a golden age;
Nostalgia, turning back a page;
Which will it be: the past or future
Into which we carve a suture...
Penury among the classes.
Poverty among the masses;
Atmospheric poison gasses
C'mon...let's everybody raise their glasses!

Politicians sell us down the river;
Then they shrug...it makes you shiver;
A corpse without the slightest quiver...
But at the "virus express"

They do deliver!!
Young people who need to be seen!

Or there won't be a smiling Mr. Clean;
Instead...you hear a silent scream

It's pandemic time at Halloween!

Bud Light

halloween as it was, and this year

impertinently knocking on death's door,
riding the rafts of fantasy,
darting,
as night melded with day,
between
the darkness and the light,
the youngest and most gleeful among us
tore through the quiet streets,
a tumble of magpies, a jabber of blackbirds,
playing gap-toothed grinning tag with doom,
intent and insistent on
treats,
just beyond
the gauntlet of fear.

this year,
just the fear.

Mary Susan Gast

Total U.S. deaths from COVID-19: 231,432

Sunday, November 1, 2020
For the people

Jeremiah's Summons*

*In which the prophet is called to speak for God,
who is justice and compassion.*

*There is something like a burning fire
shut up in my bones*
   Something that blazes hot,
   That fevers my soul,
   If I say I will not speak any more
   in the name of the Most High.

I am weary with holding it in, and I cannot,
   This burning fire of compassion,
   This surging flame of justice,
   This zeal to melt down
   The tongs and talons of oppression,
*In the name of the Most High
Who delivers the life of the needy
from the hands of evildoers.*
   Who sets up house in our marrow
   And sears us with the call
   To *speak in the name of the Most High*
   The words of liberation,
   The lyrics of deliverance.

*Whenever I speak, I must cry out,
"Violence and destruction!"*
   For there is terror all around,
   Wildfire on a rampage,
   Devouring liberty,
   Consuming native lands,
   Choking the voices of dissent,
   Making ash of food and shelter,
   Incinerating hope.

*Whenever I speak, I must cry out,
"Violence and destruction!"*

*To You, I have committed my cause,
To You, who delivers the life of the needy
from the hands of evildoers.*

Mary Susan Gast
*Words from the Book of Jeremiah appear in italics

We the People

The sting of indifference
Shall straddle the land
Until We the People
Compose songs of commitment

When sacred lyrics
Splatter the ground like falling rain
The colors of the ripened corn
Shall bring Truth, Justice, and
Safe Journey to the people

Hang onto hope
Stay balanced in tradition
Gather holy water from sacred wells

Rejoice
Marvel the heavenly wonders
Sing the sacred songs

Jeannette DesBoine

Total U.S. deaths from COVID-19: 232,836

96

CONTRIBUTORS

All of the contributors to Yearning to Breathe Free are multi-faceted people of diverse interests. Here we offer the briefest pictures of these poets and authors, including where they lived in 2020 and what occupations, other than writing, they pursued that year. If they've published a book, we note that, too.

Dee Allen., Oakland CA. Latest book: *Elohi Unitsi: Poems [2013-2018]*.

Sandra Anfang, Petaluma CA, teacher and editor. Author of *Xylem Highway*.

Jerry Bolick, Brisbane CA.

Peter Bray, Benicia handyman and newspaper columnist. Most recent book: *Pieces of Work*.

Genea Brice, Vacaville CA, inaugural Poet Laureate of Vallejo CA. Child advocate. Most recent book: *A Way with Words: Poems, Prose, and Other Masterpieces, Book 1*.

Mary Brown, Vallejo CA. CEO Optimal Fitness.

Suzanne Bruce, Fairfield CA. Author of *Her Visions, Her Voices*.

Lauren Coodley, Napa CA, local historian. Most recent book is *Lost Napa Valley*.

Cathy Dana, past Poet Laureate of Alameda CA, hypnotherapist and body worker. Author of *My Dad Believed in Love*.

Jeannette DesBoine, El Sobrante CA, spent 2020 in El Paso TX. Latest books: *A Diary of Morning Prayers* and *The Meeting*.

Mary Eichbauer, Benicia. Her recently published book of poetry is *After the Opera*.

Johanna Ely, a past Poet Laureate of Benicia. Her latest book is *Postcards from a Dream*.

Will Emes, Jr., Benicia. Building construction, maintenance, and design.

Tamar Enoch, Walnut Creek CA, speech therapist.

James Fredenburg, Suisun City CA. Current book: *Reflections on a Leaf Floating*.

Deborah L. Fruchey, Walnut Creek, CA, writer and editor. Most recent book: *Three Kinds of Dark*.

Mary Susan Gast, Benicia's current Poet Laureate.

Carol Gieg, Benicia. Author of *TBI—To Be Injured, Surviving and Thriving After a Brain Injury*.

Beth Grimm, Benicia. Most recent book: *Great Grandpa Chronicles*.

Brandon Greene, civil rights attorney living in Benicia.

Evie Groch, El Cerrito CA. Fieldwork Supervisor for New Administrators in Education. Forthcoming book: *Half the Hurricanes*.

Deborah Grossman, past Poet Laureate of Pleasanton CA.

Laurie Hailey lives in Walnut Creek.

Mary Harrell, Andover MN.

Diana Helmuth, Oakland CA. Her recent book is *How to Suffer Outside: A Beginner's Guide to Hiking and Backpacking*.

Kathleen Herrmann, Vallejo CA, Elementary Education Volunteer.

Sherilee Hoffmann, Benicia. Speaker on wellness.

Georgette Howington, Martinez, conservationist with California Bluebird Recovery Program.

Joanne Jagoda, Oakland CA. Author of *Runaway Hourglass, Seventy Poems Celebrating Seventy Years*.

Shirley King, Benicia.

Charles Kruger, Vallejo CA, editor and painter.

Galen Kusic, Editor of the *Benicia Herald*.

Mary Beth Lamb, Pacheco CA, Administrative Assistant, Jesuit School of Theology.

D.L. Lang, past Poet Laureate of Vallejo CA. Author of *This Festival of Dreams*.

Ramona Lappier, Martinez CA.

Ronna Leon, past Poet Laureate of Benicia.

Aqueila M. Lewis-Ross, Las Vegas NV. *Oakland Voices* correspondent. Author of *Stop Hurting and Dance.*

Bud Light, El Cerrito CA. Most recent book: *Marking Time.*

Cooky Longo, Benicia.

Juanita Martin, inaugural Poet Laureate of Fairfield CA. New book: *Quiet Intensity.*

Katrina Monroe, Benicia. Author of *Transitions and Reinventions.*

Bruce Moody, Berkeley CA. Book forthcoming: *Water, A Story in Stories.*

Deborah Morrison, Benicia, monarch butterfly conservationist.

Myra Nissen, Benicia, alternative health care practitioner and homeopath.

Krista O'Connor, Petaluma CA, Educator at Petaluma High School.

Carolyn Plath, Benicia.

James Quinn, Benicia. Elementary School Teacher, Tutor, Writer for *Local Happenings* and *Vallejo Magazine.*

Jan Radesky, Benicia, fabric artist.

Lois Requist, past Poet Laureate of Benicia. Latest book: *Late Harvest Green.*

Bobby Richardson, Benicia.

Alyza Lee Salomon, Hercules CA. Dancer with Poetic Dance Theater Company.

Deborah Bachels Schmidt, El Sobrante CA. Music teacher. Upcoming book: *Stumbling into Grace.*

Nina Serrano, Vallejo CA. Radio host. Most recent book of poetry: *Heart Strong.*

Sherry Sheehan, Crockett CA. Latest book: *Across Currents*, with painter Robert Chapla.

Thomas Stanton, past Poet Laureate of Benicia, composer, visual artist, performance artist.

Roger Straw, Benicia resident, publisher of *The Benicia Independent.*

Shawna Swetech, Forestville CA, Registered Nurse.

Diana Tenes, San Jose, CA. Creator of card game "Get Your Happy."

Ryleigh Todd, Benicia Middle School student.

Nancy Tolin, Benicia, visual artist and designer.

Bella Vaca, student at Petaluma Junior High School.

Becky Bishop White, Benicia. Most recent book: *Poetry Salad.*

Joseph L. Wilder, Benicia. Financial Advisor.

Leonore Wilson, past Napa County Poet Laureate. Most recent book: *Tremendum, Augustum.*

Index by Author

104

Index by Title

CPSIA information can be obtained
at www.ICGtesting.com
Printed in the USA
LVHW060052110522
718323LV00013B/366

9 781735 499925